WICHITA STATE BASEBALL COMES BACK

GENE STEPHENSON AND THE MAKING OF A SHOCKER CHAMPIONSHIP TRADITION

JOHN E. BROWN

FOREWORD BY JOE CARTER,
INTRODUCTION BY GENE STEPHENSON

Charleston — London

THE
History
PRESS

Published by The History Press
Charleston, SC 29403
www.historypress.net

Copyright © 2014 by John E. Brown
All rights reserved

First published 2014

Manufactured in the United States

ISBN 978.1.62619.382.6

Library of Congress CIP data applied for.

CONTENTS

FOREWORD

I magine you've just been given the keys to a brand-new car—but you have to build the car yourself. You don't have all the parts to build it, but you were expected to have it built and running yesterday.

This is the story of the coach who built one of the top college baseball programs in the nation from the ground up in just a few short years. Gene Stephenson took Wichita State University baseball from a Volkswagen to a BMW in no time at all. With no practice facilities, no bleachers, no players and, most importantly, no money, Gene embarked on a mission that he would absolutely not allow to fail.

In 1979, my freshman year, we had to practice indoors at the local Northside YMCA. We alternated our running between the sides of the indoor swimming pool at the Y and—after 11:00 p.m.—on the concourse of Henry Levitt Arena. Did we complain? No. Gene would never let us complain.

Our goal was to put the Wichita State baseball program on the map. Boy did we ever! In 1979, we racked up sixty-five wins and broke or tied eight NCAA single-season team offensive records. Offense was our game, and we had the best general to lead us. It didn't matter that there were no bleachers at the field and no locker rooms in which to dress (we had to dress in our cars.) We played double-headers every time we played, and we loved it. After just two short years, the Shockers were off and running.

The teaching ability of Gene and his coaching staff took me from being just another "raw" athlete to being the second player drafted overall in the

1981 Major League draft. I owe all my success in the Majors to Gene and my teammates; they got me ready.

Go Shockers!

—JOE CARTER

ACKNOWLEDGEMENTS

The black-and-white images in this book appear through the kind consideration of the Special Collections and Archives of Wichita State University Libraries, where Mary Nelson worked industriously to ensure specifications and meet deadlines. All other photos come from the Office of Media Relations at Wichita State University (a special thanks to Tami Cutler) and from the personal collection of Coach Gene Stephenson.

INTRODUCTION

I was happy at the University of Oklahoma in 1977. I had as good a job with as much potential as ever a young coach might want. At its best, the Wichita State position was a risk, and at its worst, it was an impossible task. Frankly, all my friends—including fellow coaches, Major League scouts and family members—advised strongly against it. But opportunities like that don't come along very often, and I wanted to build something great from nothing. Where people who cared about me saw crazy impossibility, I saw a chance—a chance that, with enough hard work, might pay off in an exceptional opportunity for some young men whom other baseball programs had ignored or failed to develop fully.

Facing seemingly insurmountable obstacles at all turns (including little money; no bats, balls or uniforms; no field; no history of baseball success; a cold climate; and minimal support from the university's administration), we set about making Wichita State baseball a top Division I program.

Looking back, I feel no resentment due to broken promises. Nor do I wish that one thing about those years might have been different—except less stress on our family. And from the bottom of my heart, I thank all the kind, gracious people who supported the team when every dollar mattered.

A few months ago, a sportswriter for the *Daily Oklahoman* called the resurrection of baseball at Wichita State "the greatest baseball story every told." Well, maybe it is. Read on and decide for yourself.

—GENE STEPHENSON

Chapter 1

$1,000 A MONTH AND FREE LONG DISTANCE

N ew WSU Baseball Coach Pledges Winning Team" read the headline of February 12, 1977, in the morning's edition of the *Wichita Eagle*. It was a pretty typical thing for a new coach to say—but this wasn't your typical new coach.

Two days earlier, Gene Stephenson, at thirty-one years of age, had been chosen as the man to bring baseball back to Wichita State University after a seven-year leave of absence. The *Eagle* dutifully reported that seventy-six applicants had come forward seeking the position that Stephenson had just won.

Well, maybe.

College athletics, especially a second-tier NCAA sport such as baseball, operated by a different set of assumptions back then. Standard operational procedures in collegiate sports programs had not yet bent to the whims of high finance. Big money had not yet made its presence felt (at least officially), and so the coaching profession, like the lives of the players it recruited, was far less controlled by rabid alumni in search of bragging rights at the country club and far less nomadic in the firing of good men, teachers of the game who failed to win sufficiently often, sufficiently soon.

In 1977, football and basketball remained the marquee collegiate sports. Notre Dame beat Texas and Heisman running back Earl Campbell in the Cotton Bowl to win the national championship, and even then the polling method of selecting a champion was generating its heat and its fury, as five schools finished with identical 11-1 records. NCAA basketball involved just thirty-two teams in its championship tournament in 1977, the last year in which teams were not seeded. Butch Lee led Marquette to a 67–59 win over North Carolina in Coach Al McGuire's last game to win the championship on the court, as opposed to in the offices of the Associated Press. Meanwhile, over in Charleston, the Panthers of Eastern Illinois University were celebrating their NCAA championship in cross-country, and only a precious few more sports fans will remember that Coach Jim Brock showed Arizona State to a 2–1, final-game win over South Carolina in the 1977 College World Series in Omaha, the series still in its old double-elimination format. Collegiate baseball took a decided third or fourth seat in the stadiums of the National Collegiate Athletic Association (NCAA), its best players as much the provenance of the American and National Leagues as of the alma maters in the meantime.

That said, by 1977, collegiate baseball had begun a modern legacy. It had seen its great players go on to Hall of Fame careers in the Major Leagues, as well as the refinements of the game and the more systematic development of players at ever-younger ages. By 1977, NCAA baseball already recognized a few legendary coaches—virtually all of them at warm-weather, big-time schools—including Bobby Winkles at Arizona State, Cliff Gustafson at Texas and Jerry Kindall at Arizona. But none was more recognized than USC's Rod Dedeaux, who by 1977 had won seven College World Series—including five in a row from 1970 to 1974—and who would win it again a year later, in 1978. Only Dick Siebert at Minnesota had shown the southern schools that champions sometimes played on frozen infields.

In late 1973, Rod Dedeaux was sitting in his Southern California office when the phone rang. It was University of Oklahoma's Gene Stephenson on the line, and he was wondering if the national champions would like to come to Norman to play the Sooners, who were growing their own rich baseball tradition. Such was the confidence in the young voice at the other end of the line.

Gene had shared in what he describes as "great success" at the University of Oklahoma, five years (1972–77) in which the Sooners had made successive appearances at the College World Series in Omaha. These were days in which collegiate baseball coaches found jobs and stayed put, days in which desirable sorts of openings came along infrequently at best. Oklahoma's head coach, Enos Semore, had shown remarkable confidence in his young assistant, assigning Gene responsibilities typically reserved for the head coach. In his tenure in Norman, Gene scheduled the Sooners' games for the coming season. He recruited. He worked with the scouts of every Major League team, shepherding teenaged prospects into a program that would teach again and again the basics of hitting, throwing, pitching, baserunning and fielding and that would show a talented center fielder how to become a component of a team on its way to Omaha. Gene organized all team travel. He became involved in fundraising, alumni relations and all the other non-baseball endeavors of running a baseball team.

No one should accuse Gene Stephenson of being brash. At the same time, however, no one should find him in any way shy or shrinking. Told to schedule the strongest season he could muster, he simply called up Mr. Rod Dedeaux, the man who had won more collegiate baseball championships than any other coach and the builder of the strongest program in the history of the amateur sport. Gene had met Dedeaux once before in Germany in 1970, when Gene was commander of the midnight duty train through the East German corridor while serving in the U.S. Army. So, Gene called up and asked if Rod wanted to play in Norman, and college baseball's greatest coach said, "Sure. Why not?"

Gene had continued to develop his innate sense of toughness at OU. It was a natural aggressiveness that found expression first in the rough-and-tumble life of a small Okie town, then in collegiate athletics as a baseball and football player at Missouri, then in the military and, finally, under Coach Semore, whom Gene described as "a hardworking guy [who is] really committed to being excellent in every way. He's an honest man, straight up…good as they come." At the time, Coach Semore was halfway through his twenty-year tenure in Norman and had won 851 games.

Naturally, Coach Semore could not understand why his protégé would up and leave as he did. The move simply made no sense. The arguments for staying were strong: the Oklahoma program was sending teams year after year to the College World Series, pay raises were regularly forthcoming, Gene had more responsibility and concomitant authority than perhaps any other assistant coach in the country and Barry Switzer had even hired Gene to help in the football team's recruiting efforts. The arguments for going were, well, a challenge. "At OU, I was making $25,000 and was given a new car every six months, free clothes and football tickets," recalls Gene. "We were living large."

ONE FREE NIGHT AT THE HILTON INN

Wichita State University had attempted a resurgence of baseball in 1973, when Jeff Pentland arrived on campus. Hired as an assistant athletic director and brought in from Ted Bredehoft's Arizona State University, he came with the intent of becoming head coach of a resurrected program. He and athletic director Bredehoft had puttered ahead, the media attention and donor support focused on a winning basketball team and a football team that limped along in the sad years following the 1970 tragedy in the Colorado mountains when a plane carrying players and coaches crashed near Silver Plume, killing thirty-one people. By the 1975–76 school year, would-be coach Pentland left in frustration, the likelihood of a WSU baseball program slipping, in his mind, toward impossibility.

When the designated-hitter approach failed to produce the beginnings of baseball, the WSU athletic department reverted to the conventional methods of hiring an NCAA Division I coach. Most of the applicants fled in terror after hearing the budget figure: $50,000 for the whole shebang—salaries, recruiting, scholarships, field, equipment, uniforms, travel, you name it.

"I'm not at all sure I was the top guy," Gene says today. "But I had so much confidence, so much belief that anything was possible. I simply refused to listen to those people who told me I was out of my mind to leave Oklahoma for a school with no baseball tradition in a second-tier league with a cold climate." Strike three.

Invited to an in-person interview, Gene found himself spending a night at the Hilton Inn East, wondering what in the world he had ventured upon. "Wichita seemed to be a good town with some possibilities that might be yet untapped," he recalls. "I had a family to support though, and the $1,000 a month WSU was offering didn't leave me much choice. No way could I take a pay cut with a wife and two kids." The review committee did not offer Gene the job immediately. Coach Semore wanted him to stay at OU, and he told him so often and loudly. Still, the thought of starting a program from nothing hung around, asserted itself at odd hours and made Gene think that maybe baseball could flourish on the WSU campus once more.

Were you to ask him now—after all the wins, all the records, all the players sent to the Big Leagues and the hundreds more sent into lives of character and purpose—Gene Stephenson will tell you that maybe he was "the best of what was left in a process of elimination," a gambler, an old boy willing to look down a dead-end road and see a sign pointing straight to Omaha. "I knew that, with the relationships we had built with pro scouts, some recruits might at least take a look at Wichita State," he says. "I can't say that I was actually excited about our prospects. We had no players, no field and no money."

But he came anyway, for a smaller salary and fewer employee benefits, from one of America's premier baseball schools to build a program, in terms both literal and figurative, from the ground up. "The big fun lay in starting from scratch," Gene recalls. "I really felt that the city would respond to big ambitions, would want to share in the excitement of baseball coming back to town. The process in those days called for pro scouts to identify the talent and then to help guide prospects into schools where their skills could be seasoned." The universities might also need to address a young man's character, his attitudes toward life in general, teaching along the way the discipline, persistence and willingness to work necessary to play at the next level. "To some degree, we expected to take marginal students at WSU, marginal characters, and turn them into good men and productive citizens." He was absolutely certain that he could find the players necessary for a trip to Rosenblatt Stadium someday, that he could mold them into a team with a collective heart and mind not unlike his own.

In his first press conference, a hard-charging Stephenson (sans mustache and sporting a full head of curly, dark hair) predicted that he would produce "winning teams" for a salary of $1,000 a month on a month-to-month contract, a meager sum compared to what he'd been receiving as an assistant coach at tradition-rich Oklahoma. His next claim could not have been more unequivocal, more specific or more ridiculous: "In four years, we're going to challenge for the College World Series." By now, the local sports community was used to the proclamations and the promotions of athletic director Ted Bredehoft, and promises were not necessarily meant to be kept. Not every wild boast need come true around Cessna Stadium.

But Gene Stephenson could not have been more sincere—or more serious.

Looking back at his decision to come north to Kansas, Gene said, "I had a passion, and I knew that we were going to make it successful. This was a huge risk, but honestly, I just never entertained the thought that we would fail. Sure, I saw some risk. But I saw way more opportunity. Success is ultimately a matter of what you are willing to put into the job. Still, people shook their heads at my decision. They told me that it simply could not be done, told me that I was a crazy, crazy man."

Well-Nigh Impeccable

The naysayers' logic was sound. Kansas's population was small, the pool of available players made smaller still by the fact that only 8 percent of all Kansas high schools played baseball. In 1977, the best of the graduates from those few prep programs naturally turned their attentions toward the University of Kansas and Kansas State University, both members of the athletically prestigious Big Eight Conference. But still Gene believed. "I was a very confident, prepared coach from my experience with Enos. I had been given a lot of responsibilities because he had faith in me. And I had this unbelievable, burning desire to be a head coach." Bredehoft reported after the fact that "fourteen Major League scouts gave Gene high marks. They were so confident in his ability to build a program to which big-league teams would guide their top prospects for four years of seasoning."

On East Douglas, on the second floor of the daily newspaper, in a time when cigarette smoke still hung over the manual typewriters of the columnists who stabbed at them, Bill McKay wrote in his first piece after Stephenson's hiring, "He brings with him coaching and recruiting credentials well-nigh impeccable." Those were days in which "well-nigh" still rang forth from the *Wichita Eagle*'s sports pages, days in which even the most grizzled sportswriter might still, if he wanted, alliterate. They were also days in which a first-time head coach believed that he could build a team from the "two hundred or so quality players I had my eye on," players evenly divided between the region's—no, the nation's—junior college and high school ball teams. "We need seven or eight players in key positions," Gene told the paper. "I'll surround them with walk-ons. I need three pitchers who can win, a catcher, two infielders, and one outstanding outfielder." With those ingredients, he was sure that "we can surprise a lot of people. And we won't have any trouble scheduling games, because other teams will think that we'll be an easy win. And right away, I want KU and K-State on the schedule." The young coach, for all his exuberance and his will to win, did not want (at least not immediately) to see in the batter's box the crimson-and-cream of the university he had just left. But there was no fear there—just respect. Respect for Coach Enos Semore, the man who had given him just about everything.

As a last indication that there were no hard feelings, Coach Semore let Gene bring his desk to Wichita. A dark hulk of indefinite tonnage and uncertain manufacture, the desk, with a thirty-dollar list price, came up Interstate 35 as the most expensive of his baseball possessions. So, up in Wichita, he had a favorite old desk to slide into his brand-new office under the football stadium's west-side seats, in the football team's film room, directly below the Shocker Mountain Ski School. On his door was a handmade sign: "Gene Stephenson, Head Baseball Coach." Coach Stephenson still works from that desk. It now has a new Formica top, but its legs show the warp of prolonged dampness and the stains indicating the high-water marks when the rain ran in under the door of the film room—the same door through which Gene would have to depart every time the football team wanted to review game films, the more disrespectful of the players pulling his sign off the door and fairly well stomping it again into the mudded-up asphalt.

Gene brought a baseball from Norman as well, the first ball ever to be used in his new program. It had been signed by the OU bat girls, and it sits on perhaps the homeliest desk in college baseball.

MULTITASKING AS A WAY OF LIFE

Tuesday, March 1, 1977, proved to be a typical late winter Kansas day, the wind blustering at twenty-one miles an hour, making the forty-six-degree late afternoon high seem much less comfortable.

On his first day as an NCAA Division I head coach, Gene Stephenson had broken a sweat shortly after sunup, as he began his solo career as recruiter/ fundraiser/groundskeeper/purchasing agent/cajoler/chief financial officer/ guidance counselor/equipment manager/scheduler/juggler/public servant/ utility infielder. "I was living in the Holiday Inn East," Gene remembers, "not that my living quarters mattered much. I was never there, except to grab five or six hours of sleep. The eighteen-hour days began immediately; [they were] tough times, but good times. I was doing exactly what I'd always wanted to do." At the same time, Gene was of course continuing his responsibilities as husband/father/house hunter. "Our daughter turned four a week after I started in Wichita, and our son was six at the time. Naturally, I couldn't bring our family to town until I'd found a house. And because it was so late in the school year, Paula and I decided to wait until early summer for the actual move. We were also worried about our ability to find financing. And so I'd watch the residential real estate ads day to day until I found this little place on North Parkwood on a dead-end dirt road next to Turner's Pasture with an asking price of $50,000. I figured we'd need to borrow about $45,000 to make the deal work—if we were able to get our own asking price back in Norman." In time, a baseball fanatic named Larry Foley, himself an old OU ballplayer and sponsor of a local semiprofessional team, stepped forward to help Gene and Paula obtain their loan. At roughly the same time, the largest financial supporter of Wichita State's athletic programs promised Gene nothing more than a truce: "I won't help you, but I won't hurt you either," the backer offended by the athletic director's refusal to fire an increasingly unpopular basketball coach.

Because Paula needed the family vehicle to get to work and transport the kids to school, Gene went begging at Wichita's car dealerships for a courtesy car. He was well into double figures on flat-out rejections before Steve Hull Ford came forward with a Mustang, a little low-horsepower Mustang that proudly flew the black and gold. And right away, weekends with his family disappeared from Gene's schedule. He quickly put together a list of necessary equipment—uniforms at the top, bats and balls midway down and socks and jockstraps at the end—and went to lunch with Mr. L.C. Harmon, a big-hearted, friendly and generous man who pointed directly at the bottom of Gene's itemized list. The poverty-stricken coach thought to himself, "Well, socks and supporters are better than nothing." But Gene was mistaken. Mr. Harmon's pointing finger meant that he was about to purchase every single piece of equipment on the list. And Wichita State baseball was off and running.

Responsible for every last detail of planning, every last bit of doing, Gene made friends with Bill Wiesen at the Coleman Company, Wichita's world-famous manufacturer of outdoor recreation products. Bill's big contribution to WSU baseball came in the loan of his WATS (Wide-Area Telephone Service) line. In those days, telephone companies assessed their long-distance charges by the minute, with a variable rate schedule dependent on the time of day during which the call was placed. Rates were cheapest on the nights and weekends, hours when little business was done. The WATS line functioned with a bulk rate that greatly reduced the overall costs of long-distance dialing, and so Gene would come down to Coleman's offices in the company's historic headquarters on Wichita's East Second Street five or six nights a week, and he would commence the purposeful dialing of numbers belonging to the families of ballplayers who most certainly had never heard of him or, very likely, his new employer.

Gene backed down from nobody. He called up Bill Gullickson, drafted by the Montreal Expos in June 1977 as the second overall pick in the Major League Baseball draft, and asked if Bill would like to refine his pitches on the mound in Wichita. He called Terry Francona in New Brighton, Pennsylvania, and talked to him at such length and with such persuasion that the eventual manager of the Boston Red Sox narrowed his collegiate choices down to the sandbur-filled empty lot at Wichita State and the groomed, hallowed diamond of the University of Arizona. "We went after everybody," Gene says, "and we used any means the rules allowed. We really thought we were going to get Ron Gardenhire [who would go on to be an All-American at the University of Texas, a five-year infielder with the New York Mets and Minnesota Twins and, presently, the Twins' manager] when he graduated from Eastern Okmulgee [a junior college in Oklahoma]. He came up to Wichita to see his girlfriend, and we rushed him pretty hard."

Gene had signed Rick Sutcliffe to a national letter of intent at Oklahoma two years previous, but the six-foot-seven Sutcliffe took his fastball directly to the Dodgers. Since Rick could not possibly pitch for the Shockers, Gene asked Sutcliffe to come to Wichita to speak to the team.

During his recruitment process, Coach Stephenson noted that "good people matter much more than material things," an argument far less obvious than a first read might suggest. He simply—and correctly—believed that good people attract other good people, that good parents are necessarily more concerned about the quality of their sons' coaching, in terms both moral and athletic, than the quality of the infield grass.

"HI, I'M GENE STEPHENSON."

It's June in Kansas in 1977, and the wind-blown, one-hundred-degree heat is settling in. "Every day, every single day, I'm pounding the pavement. I'm walking up to every prospect in sight, introducing myself and asking for a walk-on. I'm talking to local high school coaches. I'm looking at every kid on the field, for whatever reason, at West Side Athletic. In those days, if a player had graduated from high school, he was eligible. And I found some talent, all right. Honestly, they maybe weren't smartest kids on the block, and some had a few character issues that needed to be addressed."

With about $6,000 in scholarship money floating around for the entire first season, Gene had to be circumspect in those hamstrung, late evening phone calls to recruits. On the one hand, he had to sing of the opportunities waiting for the young third baseman, were he to sign a letter of intent with Wichita State, opportunities that amounted to "a chance to play your freshman year against top-flight opponents." On the other hand, he could promise tangible financial assistance only in the form of a likely Pell Grant (which, luckily, did not have to be repaid), the federal monies available to low-income student-athletes. Unable to visit his recruits and unable to offer them a fraction of the enticements waiting in Austin or Los Angeles or back in Norman, he used his friends, the pro scouts, to help sell the start-up program. These scouts would counsel parents to entrust their sons to Gene Stephenson, who would help them become better ballplayers and, perhaps more importantly, better men. And once a prospect had warmed to the idea of a visit to campus, Gene would scurry in search of a local businessman who might be willing to put an airline ticket on his credit card. (As a matter of fact, Gene never once recruited with a full complement of scholarships until he went after the 1989 recruiting class.) Of course, NCAA rules forbade tryouts. Enrollment had to come first, and so Gene was forced to recruit second hand, the scouts his roving eyes on the sandlots and high school fields of the nation.

THE FIRST GOOD PEOPLE

"We are beginning what will be one of the outstanding college baseball programs in the country." Thus read the first sentence of Gene Stephenson's first written contact with a prospective baseball player at Wichita State University for the 1977–78 academic year. No qualification. No subjunctive mood. No sense of mere probability. "What will be one of the outstanding college baseball programs in the country." Not "what might be," "what might very well be" or "what, with a little luck, could be"—instead it was "what *will* be."

As if by the strong and repeated assertion of his supreme confidence in his players (players yet to be named, by the way) and his ability to teach and to motivate them, Coach Gene Stephenson was going to keep an unequivocal, out-loud and here-we-come promise to challenge for a berth in the College World Series in four—count 'em—four years. The coach was willing to make a slight concession to the nature of reality in his second sentence, where the leadoff dependent clause admitted that "the Shockers do not have a great baseball tradition." "But the ingredients are here," Gene insisted, as long as the ingredients did not include a diamond of one's own, a full roster of scholarships, salaries for assistant coaches or first dibs on a practice field. Let no one suggest that Gene Stephenson ever saw a glass anything less than half full. With a straight face, as nearly as a casual passerby might tell, Gene wrote to his chosen youngsters, "The ingredients are here." And among the parts of a winning program that truly do count, indeed they were. "Professional baseball and its scouts like to see young men go into good, sound college baseball programs," he wrote. "The trouble is that there are simply not enough good college programs for potential pro prospects to enter." So Gene was busy contacting his scout friends, the salty dogs who knew where the talent lay, obscured perhaps by piney woods or an inner-city neighborhood's grit and stink. The scouts knew the youngsters not ready—for whatever reason, whether it be refinement of skills, knowledge of the game, grades or maybe a rap sheet—for the big Division I schools, the established programs. The scouts knew such youngsters as might find a home amid the talcumed dirt of a program born but not yet alive.

Gene had seen enough of Wichita and its baseball fans to promise his first-year recruits a commitment "to the goal of competing for a berth in the College World Series and a possible National Championship!" The man did aim high. He brought others along, in just a few months demonstrating the infectious nature of his enthusiasm for and his unflappable confidence in the power of positive thinking. As he would quickly remind his players, "However, like all things worth attaining, that will not come easy. It will take (1) great players who are dedicated to being the best, (2) fine facilities where players can practice to improve their skills to their fullest potential, (3) financial backing in order to sustain a top-flight program and (4) lots and lots of practice both mentally and physically all year round." Gene remained in full, year-round management of ingredients 1 and 4, his fatherly discipline a given, his demands for performance on and off the field beyond argument and his willingness to hold his players to his own work ethic already proven.

The second and third ingredients were not so easily managed, though, as they darted and feinted across a weeded-up outfield, out past anyone's ability to predict much less control. But Gene Stephenson believed.

A Color Television in Every Lounge

The new coach reached far into the university's catalogue to locate such enticement as he might offer a recruit. Good gosh, he wrote about the dormitory, Fairmount Towers, "a housing, recreational, and dining complex as good as any in the country today." Remembering, of course, that the physical attractions available in 1977 represent the technology of the time, it still occurred to Coach Stephenson to cite Fairmount's central heat and air-conditioning, its carpeting and the convenience and comfort of its layout—"a bathroom shared between every two rooms, large spacious living quarters, and a color television in the lounge of every floor." The outdoor swimming pool sold well, too.

He wrote of a weight room, a large new sauna bath and an indoor practice facility—"all available for use by our athletes." As he was soon to discover himself, the indoor practice facility was available for use only by athletes who happened to be playing basketball. Contrary to all logic, all common sense and every word of the promises made him at his hiring, the athletic department decided that the on-campus arena would remain the sole property of the roundballers. No baseball players need attempt entry, even though in all good conscience, telling the absolute truth as he knew it, Gene informed his players that "by next winter, we will have a batting cage inside Henry Levitt Arena to use for any cold-weather workouts. The warmth of the arena will aid us considerably during the winter." Prohibited, for reasons known only to WSU administrators, from practicing in Henry Levitt Arena, the 1978 Shockers put on their sweats and ran, north into the wind, to a YMCA on Hillside Avenue, two miles or so up the street from those spacious living quarters in Fairmount Towers.

For players from Kansas and states farther north, who were used to playing fifteen, maybe sixteen games in their high school careers, Gene promised an essentially endless summer. "At Wichita State, there is <u>NO</u> [caps and underlining Gene's] limit as to the number of games we can play. In our opening season, we hope to have a 65- to 70-game schedule against teams from the Big Eight, Big Ten, Southwest Conference, Missouri Valley, leading independents and others. Our ultimate goal is to play the nation's finest college teams each year and to be competitive with them." And again with the facilities, he assured recruits that "in the very near future, we plan on playing some of our more important games in Lawrence Stadium, site of National Baseball Congress tournament in August and home of the Chicago Cubs' Triple-A affiliate, the Wichita Aeros." Their coach was inviting these young players to imagine themselves in the bottom of the ninth in a Triple-A ballpark full of National League scouts just waiting to hand them a lucrative contract with a huge signing bonus. In Gene Stephenson's mind, it never hurts to dream, but practice starts again tomorrow with calisthenics of which the U.S. Marine Corps might approve.

Gene touted the growth of the university and its "expansion of its educational opportunities," the diversity of the student body ("almost 16,000 students from nearly every state in the Union and from 37 foreign countries") and its size, which was "large enough to command outstanding facilities yet small enough to treat students as individuals, with a faculty committed to their students and their aspirations." He quickly turned then to scholarships, and perhaps the only genuine in-one's-face stretch-of-the-truth in his entire letter: "We believe our baseball scholarship program is as good as any other school in the country at this time. We can give a FULL [yep, capitalization Gene's] scholarship; however, we will split most scholarships." OMG, as Gene's players today might type. OMG. With barely $6,000 to split among the entire team, he knew that his offers of financial assistance would be few—and small. And then, Gene being Gene, he added one last thought: "If an athlete comes into our program with no scholarship or a partial, we will improve his scholarship if he shows he can play." Work hard, he was saying. Come to play. Be a gamer. Take the extra base. Run in the rain.

At the end of his letter, Gene identified the lessons to be learned, the priorities to be established. And he said the word like the men who had taught him, in football and baseball alike, the coaches and the teachers who had brought him this far. "We like young men who can play baseball, but first they must be good students." As before and after practice, in the daily lectures about hitting the cutoff man and hitting the books hard and harder still, Coach Stephenson laid down the law, identifying in numerical order the way it would be. Education first, baseball second and TGIF and coeds a distant third. After class and study and baseball practice, precious little time would be left, he predicted, "for social activities." And then, in a veiled reference to what one would assume to be fraternities, he said, "We do not encourage, nor do we discourage social organizations. We leave that decision to the individual." Not exactly an endorsement of the Greek system—or the chess club, for that matter.

"I worked to establish rapport with these young players, always trying to take the conversation beyond a phone call," says Gene. "I'd encourage them to talk to the professional scouts, to ask them, 'Is this guy for real?'"

RUNNER ON THIRD, TUBA PLAYER ON FIRST

Before the first Shocker had ever put on the black-and-gold in the resurrected baseball program, Coach Stephenson was thinking Major League. "We want people to know that we're serious about producing players of professional caliber," he said. "We want baseball people to know that Wichita State intends to be a home for superb play, right from the beginning." The first practices were held at the edge of campus on an empty lot, the site of present-day Hubbard Hall, where Little League teams practiced. No backstop. No grass. No bases. Right there is the injury of the whole deal. Here's the insult: the baseball team stood third in its claim to use of the field, behind the university marching band and WSU's soccer club. It was troubling enough that a varsity sport took second place to the band, but the 1977–78 Shocker baseball team was also forced, by university fiat, to yield to the soccer club when it, too, wanted use of the field. Not a varsity soccer team at all. Nope. The club. Foreign students kicking a borrowed ball.

By the first cold weeks in the fall of 1977, Gene had worked a deal with the executive director of the Northside YMCA for regular use of its facilities. The team would drop the nets to divide the basketball court to practice hitting while the pitchers threw back and forth—no fooling—across the swimming pool. Frequented by neighborhood toughs, the locals sometimes out of control up there, the Y remained the baseball team's to borrow "only because we had bats to back up our claim to use of the facilities," says Gene.

Gene spent some time at the mimeograph machine. His heart had changed from OU crimson to Shocker gold, but his hands were purple, and he smelled of that fearful fluid that told so many pre-Xerox children that a pop quiz was on the way. He, too, gave his share of tests, written exams cranking off that mimeograph, asking about defensive throws to cut-off men. There are runners here, the ball's hit to you here, where do you throw? Where does the throw come for backup? Who's running where when the ball comes into defensive play?

Eric Namee played baseball all his life. He attended the Show Me Baseball Camp near Branson, Missouri, where Dodger scout Don Gutteridge took a long look at his speed and his ability to hit with power. With a surprisingly hard swing from a youngster of his stature, Eric muscled on an average-sized frame. He played in the outfield at Wichita North High School on a team that finished 17-1 in the spring of 1977, one game behind the powerhouse Wichita Southeast High team. On that Buffalo team were shortstop Jimmy Thomas; Doug Hoppock, an eventual offensive lineman for the Kansas City Chiefs; and Kevin Clinton, who played four years in the Boston Red Sox organization.

In the middle of the summer, Eric walked into Gene's hideout under Cessna Stadium and announced that he'd like to play ball for Wichita State University. Keith Jones, his buddy from North High, said, "Ditto, Coach." Gene invited them both to walk on, and in doing so they were emblematic of the athletes on that field where it all began again.

"Gene talked to us before and after practice. Always extremely confident, he sounded as if we were an established program," Eric remembers. "He told us we were going to be great." The players called him "Ten," his number as an Oklahoma assistant coach, and Ten preached hard work, team play, extra effort in the late innings, going to class and behaving oneself. Mickey Lashley, who

WSU players practiced the fundamentals every day. They hit, caught and threw by the book of a beautiful game.

had played for Gene at Oklahoma, took the team through calisthenics. "Lots of stretches and running—wind sprints, running around the field house, the outside of the field house, of course," Eric recalls. Looking back on those happy weeks from his law office on the top floor of Kansas's tallest office building, Eric speaks fondly and candidly of his teammates. "First of all, I was struck by the athleticism in the guys Ten had recruited—their speed and agility, their raw strength. But they were wild guys, too, partiers, and Coach was always pushing us about grades. He was like that. Relentless, with attention to every little detail. No opportunity missed. And because he pushed himself so hard, he could ask other people to do some pretty unreasonable things."

CAMPS AND OTHER COACHES

Gene also understood that credibility—demonstrated, hard-nosed credibility—came first if he were to recruit players, fans and big-time financial supporters. And so less than a year after he arrived, in February

Arizona State coach Jim Brock addressed one of Gene's early clinics, which drew Major League and collegiate greats—players and coaches alike—to Wichita.

of 1978, WSU baseball held its first coaches' clinic. And not once did Gene ever have to pay a big name to come. Not the Dodgers' Don Drysdale. Not the Cardinals' Lou Brock. Not Willie Mays, the "Say Hey Kid" himself, who circled overhead in a plane trying to land in a Wichita buried under fourteen inches of snow. Not the nationally prominent coaches like Dick Howser from the Royals or Ron Fraser from the University of Miami or Cliff Gustafson from the University of Texas, who would soon become the winningest coach in collegiate baseball history—that is, until the currently field-less Gene Stephenson passed him in a blur. Six years in a row they came to Wichita out of respect for what the team was trying to do, out of regard for Gene both personally and professionally.

Gene also brought Steve Garvey to campus. Garvey, a ten-time All Star, the 1974 National League MVP, holder of the National League record for consecutive games played (1,207), was known as "Mr. Clean"—one of the most conspicuously decent players in the game at the time. Still a Dodger in the spring of 1978, Garvey came to town to lend authority and stature to the first WSU Baseball Coaches' Clinic, a three-day affair that began on Thursday evening with Garvey's introduction at halftime of the Shocker–Tulsa Golden Hurricane basketball game in Henry Leavitt Arena. The legendary first baseman spoke at the University Forum Board lecture on Friday morning before conducting a two-hour clinic with the team at the Northside YMCA, where he announced his opinion that "hitting a baseball is the most difficult job in sports." Seven months later, Garvey would hit four home runs in the 1978 National League Championship Series, demonstrating that with enough good coaching and thousands of hours of practice, difficulties really can be overcome.

A SCHEDULE AND ITS CONSEQUENCES

Gene acknowledged that the schedule would be "demanding," especially for a first-year program, "but I do think we will have favorable results from it. One thing is for sure, with this many games, it should allow us to develop our players and pitching staff more rapidly." He had even scheduled an early May exhibition game against the Wichita Aeros, the Chicago Cubs' Triple-A American Association team, Gene eager to showcase his team in any venue anytime.

Not content with the vagueness of most "coachly" commentary, Gene predicted that by the time of the Missouri Valley Conference Baseball Championships in Omaha on May 18, his team would be "in prime competitive shape, a strong challenger for the league title." He stepped right up and announced that the Shockers would be "a proven squad ready for powers like Southern Illinois University, Tulsa, and Creighton. We want to be the conference's representative in the NCAA regionals."

Chapter 2

FOR THE LOVE OF THE GAME AND LITTLE ELSE

That first budget of $50,000 included a whopping $3,000 for an assistant coach, but Gene was able to persuade one of his former players at Oklahoma to accept the position at that meager salary. Love of the game right there, Coach Terry Jolly. The announcement came on March 17 that Jolly, just twenty-three years old, would join his old coach in Wichita. A native of Shawnee, Oklahoma, Terry was a four-year letterman, playing on those Big Eight championship teams on their way to Omaha each year. He batted .340 his senior year, pounding eight homers, and served as co-captain of the team. In an unmistakable act of faith, he turned down an offer to fill Gene's old position as assistant to Coach Enos Semore at OU. "I wanted Terry to come with me to Wichita, but I could offer him nothing beyond the opportunity to build something from nothing," Gene says. "Baseball was never about money for Terry. He wanted to be part of a program starting from scratch. He believed."

That belief translated to strong recruiting, his confidence in what was going to happen at silly-looking Shocker Field convincing to prospects and their families. His friend and boss says now, "I used to marvel at Terry, his absolute certainty in the face of so many naysayers. He was such a hard worker, so low-key and methodical about what we were doing…I came across as the crazy man." Coach Jolly worked with the outfielders and helped with the hitting instruction. And perhaps more importantly, he helped to stabilize the generalized mayhem associated with the first few Shocker teams and their barely repressed outlawry.

Instructional finesse and easy camaraderie with the players aside, Coach Terry Jolly is "one of the finest men I've ever known," according to his colleague Gene Stephenson.

Other OU ballplayers came to town to help Gene, including Jackie Parrish, a catcher who had left school his junior year after signing with the Dodgers, spending the last two years working his way through their minor-league organization. In making the announcement, Gene spoke about leadership "on and off the field," some relief definitely noticeable among the confident, assuring tones of his announcement speech, glad to have some cavalry on the way, the WSU program now definitely more than a one-man operation. "The three of us welcome the challenge," he said. And soon Mickey Lashley, drafted by the Dodgers, came to help, too, staying on until the start of spring training in the Major Leagues.

OF SCHOLARSHIPS AND SPORTSWRITING

Wichita State University sports information director Joe Yates was writing with obvious excitement on May 9, 1977, when he issued the press release reporting the reinstituted Shocker baseball program's first signing, brought off, per Joe, "in superb style." In echoes of Ol' Smitty the Eternal Sportswriter, Joe wrote, "Inked by Stephenson was George Wright from Capital Hill High School in

Oklahoma City, Oklahoma," the passive voice alone capable of suggesting the hugeness of it all. George definitely did have the stats: a .390 batting average in thirty-six games, ten home runs, "a 4.5 clocking in the 40-yard dash" and impressive fielding at either shortstop or in the outfield. Generally regarded as a top prospect in all of Oklahoma, many scouts expected George to be the first high school player from the state to be taken in the 1977 Major League draft. Gene was obviously elated at his signing but still quick to establish priorities from the outset: "We are very, very excited that George has decided to continue his education and further his baseball skills at WSU." School first, baseball second—just as Gene's recruitment letters had insisted.

You just have to love Joe Yates and his inking. In another breathless news release dated May 24, Joe continued, "Wichita State baseball coach Gene Stephenson has his new baseball program back in full swing again with the announcement of two more signees for the coming year. Inked by the first-year mentor were Bruce Alexander from Western Oklahoma Junior College and Bob Bomerito from Florissant Valley Community College." At the announcement of Bruce's signing, Coach Stephenson alerted fans that Alexander, a shortstop at Western Oklahoma, would be moving to the Shocker outfield to take advantage of his speed. As Yates told it, "Showing his 4.4 speed in the 40-yard dash is honest, Alexander also swiped 25 bases in 42 games." We learn also from the release that Bruce "stroked the ball a .391 battering average with 11 home runs and 55 runs batted in," those homers made more impressive by his five-foot-nine, 150-pound stature; that his nickname is "Magic"; and that he was president of his senior class at Chickasha High School, where he earned all-conference honors in football, basketball and baseball.

Bob Bomerito arrived on campus with similar numbers, including Missouri state high school records for hits, RBIs and stolen bases. Joe noted that after "moving over to Flo Valley, he responded with a .385 batting average and 45 RBIs, a new FVCC school record." His signing prompted Gene to more hyperbole. "According to Stephenson," Yates wrote, "both players will be instrumental in helping the Shocker baseball program to get off to a rip-roaring start," Gene going on to comment on Bruce's and Bob's "good minds for the game."

A little more than a week later, Joe Yates is back in front of his IBM Selectric to put out the word. Yes sir, Gene "has scored another coup with the announced signing of Tim Tolin from Bartlesville, Oklahoma," the third Oklahoma athlete in the first four signees. Gene was already changing Tim's collegiate position as well, moving him away from shortstop for use at third and first and in the outfield. And once more, the coach had found an all-around athlete—Tolin was an all-conference defensive back in football and played in the all-state tournament in basketball. Naturally, Gene talked about Tim Tolin in the same breath as George Wright: "Two of the top three prospects in Oklahoma, both are outstanding leaders and dedicated players, the kind our Shocker fans will enjoy watching." "Dedicated" was the key word in Genespeak.

With four players on the dotted line, Gene quickly added shortstop Dave Howard from Kansas City Wyandotte High School onto the signing list. Gene was content to leave him in that all-important position, what with Dave's .436 batting average, six home runs and eighteen RBIs in just sixteen games—all Wyandotte records. Matt Yeager, the oldest player on the 1978 roster, had attracted All-American attention at Seward County Community College, where he batted in the high .300s both years while pitching to a 4-2 record. Mitch Denson, who according to Joe Yates was "expected to be one of the aces of the Shockers mound corps," came to WSU even though he had won only six games in the 1977 season at Tyler (Texas) Junior College. However, Mitch's record began to shine in the consideration that the team won only those six games all year. In eighty-two innings, Denson had given up but nineteen hits, striking out 105 batters for a scintillating 1.03 ERA, the southpaw never giving up more than three hits in any game.

On June 29, Gene "got back into the signing picture again," the three players signed then giving him players sufficient to the fielding of an entire team. And here they came: Kurt Bradbury from Liberty, Missouri, a left-hander with a 5-1 senior-year record and a 1.47 ERA; Dave Waddell from Trinidad Junior College in Colorado, a draftee of the New York Mets with a 1.91 ERA in seventy-eight innings, giving up only thirty-seven hits while striking out seventy-five; and Ladell Thomason from McPherson, Kansas High School and Dodge City Junior College, a rangy (six-foot-three) pitcher and outfielder who hit .393 at Dodge.

With classes set to start in just six weeks, Gene continued his fevered recruiting, long hours on the telephone and nights spent down at the Coleman Company in its venerable old building. Cajoling. Wheedling. Trying to convince impressionable young men and their families that the architectural rendering in his hand—of a completed, fan-packed Shocker Field with contenders on the diamond—might actually be realized. Next to come were Frank Pena, Kevin Akenson and David Tuteral. Pena, the catcher Gene so desperately needed, was a key player in the cadre of guys who could win games from the get-go, a slugger with a .424 batting average and a third-team Junior College All-American. Akenson, who had big-game experience at both second base and in left field, was labeled by his Grossmont

Junior College (San Diego, California) coach as the best turner of double plays he had ever coached. Tuteral was a first baseman with all-around skills who had led his Muskogee, Oklahoma high school team in hits, runs scored, stolen bases, total bases and batting average at .344. Coach again addressed the intangibles of his new signees, speaking of "wanting to be a winner," "competitive spirit" and "willingness to be a leader." Knowing the obstacles—logistical and otherwise—waiting ahead for these young men, he understood that attitude, for them as for him, would mean everything.

Shocker spirits took a jump on July 18 with the next two signings: two studs named Bruce Morrison and Larry Groves. Morrison arrived all the way from Staten Island, where he was named the very best athlete at St.

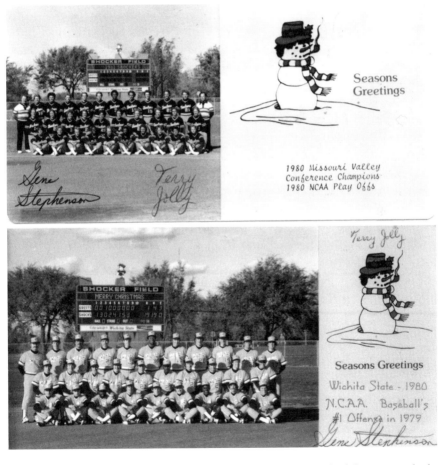

From that first pre-season onward, Gene sent a Christmas card to friends of the program, both current and prospective. It was a thoughtfulness that paid off in all sorts of ways.

Peter High School. The tallest player on the team, at six-foot-three, Bruce brought a smoking fastball to an 8-2 record with a mighty impressive 1.82 ERA. The Milwaukee Brewers had drafted Larry Groves straight out of Shawnee Mission West High School, but he wisely had foregone the minors for more seasoning, more instruction at the collegiate level. The University of Kansas had come calling, as had Missouri, most especially after he hurled a no-hitter in the state tournament his senior year at West, but he drove right through Lawrence, waving on his way to Wichita.

PAGE-ONE NEWS, LOWER-LEFT PAGE-ONE NEWS

The March rains arrived cold and nasty, and the scheduled home opener against Friends was cancelled. But the weather cleared, and three vans carrying twenty-two players and two coaches left Twenty-first Street and Hillside on Saturday, March 10. Of those players, twelve were freshmen, two were sophomores and eight were juniors, the juniors all transfers from junior colleges. The team was driving down to Texas to play seventeen games in eleven days, including six straight days of double-headers. "We could grow up a lot on this trip," said the head coach. "Or we could come home winless"—a prospect that, Gene allowed, was aging him a bit as well.

Gene drove the lead vehicle with Assistant Coach Terry Jolly piloting the last van and an unnamed but valiant driver in the middle. "I was genuinely worried that the guys in the second van might take off and never come back," Gene says. "That first-year team was the orneriest bunch of young men I have ever been around."

Sports fans in south-central Kansas turned to the *Wichita Eagle* on the morning of March 13, 1978, to learn of the previous day's most important results, and sure enough, splashed there across the first page of Section C, they read "DePaul Stages Awesome Rally"—this above the subhead "Creighton Sees Lead Transformed to Loss," the early game of the NCAA basketball tourney of evident interest to *Eagle* subscribers, Creighton being a Missouri Valley Conference school and all. And just below that lead story, those readers encountered "Soviet High Jumper Sets Indoor Record," wherein they learned that over in Italy, Vladimir Yaschanko had popped up there seven feet, eight and a half inches. Nice flop, Vladi.

Only when they followed their left forefinger down into Section C, Page One's lower quadrant, did they discover that "WSU Loses to Emporia St. in

'78 Baseball Opener." Under the byline "Special to The *Eagle*" was the first paragraph: "FORT WORTH—The Wichita State Shockers opened their 1978 baseball season here Sunday with a double-header against Emporia State. WSU dropped the opener 4–2 and was tied 4–4 in the nightcap when the game was called after 7½ innings because of darkness."

Wichita State was playing in a season-opening tournament at Texas Wesleyan University, the first of the sixty-two games Gene had scheduled. The first game began with balls—lots of balls—as Shocker starter Dave Waddell walked five of the first seven batters he faced and ESU took a 2–0 lead. In the second inning, Bob Bomerito smacked the first of his collegiate career's towering home runs, four hundred feet and more to straightaway center field. More walks and a passed ball (on a strikeout, no less) led to another Emporia State run. Waddell took the loss. Larry Groves led the Shocks at the plate, going two for three with a solo home run.

In the nightcap, Emporia State took an early 4–0 lead, but the Shocks climbed back with a solo homer from Mike Davis in the third inning and, in the seventh, tied the game with walks and timely singles from Matt Yeager and pinch hitter Kevin Akenson. Then the rains came. And the rare third slot appeared on the new team's won-loss record. WSU: 0-1-1. Good to know. But remember most: Creighton blew that big lead against DePaul.

Gene's response to his first seventeen innings as head baseball coach at Wichita State University: "I was pretty happy with our showing, considering this was our first real chance to see any action out of doors this spring." Our first real chance to see any action out of doors? The man has been charged with resurrecting a moribund athletic program at a mid-major NCAA university with a grand total of $50,000 to support that entire program for its first year, and he's happy just to be outside. "Believe me, we'll get much better," Gene said. Self-improvement evidently somehow related in baseball to practice somewhere beyond an indoor swimming pool.

The first WSU baseball victory in eight years came on March 14, 1978, when the Shockers took two from the University of Dallas by identical scores of 7–4. Three losses and an impossible tie do not exactly constitute a bad-luck streak in baseball, especially for a program playing its first games in almost a decade, but such was the competitive fire of the man that the first time his troops ran across the first-base line, he expected a win. He hadn't taken a $1,000-a-month-on-a-month-to-month-contract job for nothing. He hadn't worked eighteen-hour days for a year to absorb a loss. He wasn't about to allow that the program's few believers be rewarded with anything but win after win after win. And yet, as he would demonstrate in the most

The Shockers played with youthful exuberance and were, according to their coach, "some of the orneriest guys I've ever known."

dramatic terms possible in just a few days, Shocker baseball under Gene Stephenson was about way more than winning.

The teenagers on the 1978 team discovered early that the lectures of high school baseball, indeed of Little League, would continue in their college careers at WSU. From his playing days onward, Gene had held that the rules of the game necessarily involved lessons about the rules of a good life. For Gene Stephenson, baseball was a "carnival ride," "maybe the best, most carefree years of a young man's life," "a once-in-a-lifetime deal not to be seen again." And so before and after every practice, he talked to his players about the big abstractions, about teamwork and personal responsibility and self-discipline in the service of a greater purpose. The players were, of course, free to kick the dirt and watch the passing cars, but their coach remained relentless in his fierce assertion that baseball was life writ small or, more to Gene's point, life was baseball writ large.

With the Shocks down in Oklahoma and Texas, the team's first prolonged swing through a southern schedule demonstrated that coach meant every word of his two-a-day lectures. The *Eagle*'s Bill MacKay set the scene in his banner column of Sunday, March 26, 1978: "When I was a young and not too proficient jock, I soon learned that your typical athletic coach might make 'an example' of a player for breaking or bending a rule, but you better believe the example was never gonna be one of the guys the coach was relying on heavily to help the team win." Hold that thought.

The team was preparing for an intense three days, with three double-headers at Dan Law Field against Texas Tech, then tied with Arkansas and Houston atop the Southwest Conference. On the evening preceding the first games, junior catchers Frank Pena and Phil Cordova found just too much fun in wild west Texas, breaking curfew after a serious wingding in Lubbock, merely the most recent in a series of late nights for the pair. Gene's response was immediate and unequivocal: Frank Pena, seemingly the greater sinner, was dismissed from the team, and Phil Cordova was suspended indefinitely. Both were sent back to Wichita immediately. "I busted them good," Gene remembers. "Then I told Terry Jolly to find the slowest possible transportation home—a nasty bus ride of right at thirty-six hours."

MINIMUM REQUIREMENTS

As Bill MacKay noted in his column, "Two good catchers is the minimum requirement for a college team for whom double-headers are a way of life." And now WSU had exactly no catchers. Pena had been playing especially well, leading the team in its double-header sweep of Abilene Christian College. Casey Stengel told us, "You have to have a catcher because if you don't, you're likely to have a lot of passed balls." To their everlasting credit, three Shockers stepped forward indicating their willingness to put on the mask and chest protector, slap on the shin guards and squat behind the plate in the full intent of telling a pitcher what and where to throw. Mike Davis, the freshman infielder, allowed as how he could cut down on the passed balls. So did sophomore third baseman Bob Bomerito and junior Matt Yeager, then leading the Shockers with a .378 average, fourteen RBIs and three home runs. Matt, a rangy outfielder and sometimes short reliever from Wichita's Bishop Carroll High School, had substituted as a catcher during his two years at Seward County Community College in Liberal, Kansas. He absolutely hated the position. But he volunteered to fill the hole just the same, and his junior college experience won the job, as Gene sent seven freshmen, sophomore Bomerito and the aged junior, twenty-one-year-old Yeager, onto the diamond against the Red Raiders.

The Shockers said, "Howdy, Texas" with ten runs crossing the plate in the first inning and then coasted to an easy 14–2 blowout. The second game proved closer, much closer, but WSU prevailed 9–8. Tuesday was not so kind to the Shocker faithful. Nor was Wednesday. Tech won all four games, bringing home thirty runs in the process, a sad number of them on passed balls by the intrepid, embattled Matt Yeager and by Mike Davis, pressed into service in the final game. All due respect to both for stepping up in the face of the strong arms and frequent early season wildness of Shocker pitchers. "Matt stopped a lot of balls with his shoulders and even his throat," says Coach Stephenson. "He took a beating back there." And to the point of it all, Gene said in a post-series interview, "I don't think winning or losing had anything to do with it. If it did, I would have brought Cordova back." In the same breath, Coach made it clear that he still considered the suspended players "good kids. I care very much about the future of both young men, but I had given them several chances, and finally it came down to something being done for the sake of the team and the team's discipline. If my faith and trust in them is restored, I may bring them back. Meanwhile, it puts us in an extremely difficult position."

Meanwhile, rules remained rules. And old Gene, it seems, means what he says in those interminable talks of his.

On the long ride back to Wichita, Gene could open the scorebook and confirm what he'd suspected all along: his guys could hit, but many of them had problems with Major League–type curveballs; his pitchers had big arms and occasional big wildness—thirteen walks, for example, in one four-inning stretch; and his team wasn't sufficiently together to win most of the close ones. But he was coming back to Wichita to, at long last, introduce his guys to the homefolks.

THE ASTROTURF THAT FAILED TO ARRIVE AND THE TEAM THAT DID

Gene and his guys returned from their exodus in the American Southwest with high hopes for a home game to be played on some perfect new artificial turf. Instead they found a scoreboard, a towering Shocker-gold structure ready to report the count, hits and runs in fine and spectacular fashion. "Unfortunately," as one Wichita wag suggested, "you can't see it from McAdams Park." Some two miles south of the campus, McAdams was now to be the Shockers' home field, because only the scoreboard stood ready to go back on East Twenty-first Street; there was no turf on the infield, no fences, no warning track. There wasn't much at all really—certainly nothing approaching the $380,000 facility promised to the coach and his team and their fans.

WSU athletic director Ted Bredehoft turned the fans' attention to the Monsanto Company, the patent holder on Astroturf, the company that had also contracted with the City of Wichita for the installation of its turf at downtown's Lawrence Stadium, the company for reasons of efficiency wanting to install turf on both fields in a single continuous visit to Sedgwick County. Hence, there was a new installation date: April 1, per Monsanto. Director Bredehoft called the team to a meeting before he left town for a speaking engagement. "I think he wanted to tell them that he was proud of them, that things would get better," said Coach Stephenson, in his take on the confab. The last week in April now stood out there as the target date for Shocker Field's completion.

The headlines were inclusive: "Home Debut Successful…Shocks Sweep Iowa State." And indeed it was, and indeed they did, although the team "didn't play well," per their coach. He saw some nerves among his players "attributable to our first home game and the good turnout of fans." Eighteen games into a season, a team really should be past the jitters, but nothing about the 1978 version of the Shockers followed the norm, and so when the team followed starting pitcher Larry Groves onto the field at McAdams Park in front of four hundred fans on Monday afternoon, March 28, they heard the foreign but friendly sound of cheerful applause for the first time in a long, long while. A Wichita State baseball team had last played in front of a home crowd eight years previous, a time when these young men were just starting Little League.

Never mind, though—it was the Cyclones who suffered most from the yips, as an unearned run in the seventh, supported by five-hit pitching from Groves, carried the Shockers to a 4–3 win. And Gene Stephenson offered some tangible proof to the Wichita community that his well-traveled squad could play with older, thriving programs. Iowa State's problems persisted in the second half of the double-header when the 'Clones surrendered five unearned runs, to which Gene suggested, "We'll take them." The pitching looked solid, as Larry Groves added a complete game for a 3-0 season record. It was reassuring and then some in contrast to the just-completed Texas swing, during which the Shocker staff had given up 115 walks and 115 hits in 112 innings, the right-hander Groves the lone exception to the run-fest, as he went 2-0 in Texas with an immaculate 1.29 ERA against Lone Star batters.

Control remained a distant second to raw, ballistic arm speed among Shocker pitchers' early season strengths. Groves's 2.14 ERA glistened in its own right but seemed scintillating indeed in comparison to a team ERA approaching 6.00. The mound staff refused to blame the weather or the conditions of their daily practices, however. Larry spoke for his fellow pitchers when he said, "I don't see much difference between throwing inside or outside. We have a portable pitching mound that we use." Larry Groves diplomatically neglected to mention that the mound was sometimes set up at the North Branch YMCA on one side of the swimming pool, with the catcher on the far side of the sky-blue water.

"I chose Wichita State because I had faith in Coach Stephenson," Larry said outright. In further keeping with Gene's making the best use of the talent he had recruited, Groves traded out DH and first-base duties with Bruce Morrison, the New Yorker who could pitch and hit big-time. Matt Yeager and Mike Davis were sharing catching duties in place of the still-suspended curfew-breakers, Davis rotating between shortstop and second base as well. The remaining Wichita North High School walk-on, Keith Jones, was showing himself more than able in centerfield in place of Bruce Alexander and his leg injury, while Kevin Akenson was seeing action at second as Davis played elsewhere.

On the following Wednesday, the *Wichita Eagle* published another seventy-two-point headline about the resurgent team: "Shocks Win Two; Davis Hits 4 HRs," a two-column lead into a detailed story written by staffer Russ Corbitt detailing exactly how "shortstop Mike Davis and the Wichita State Shockers had one of those days you dream about Tuesday as they swept a baseball double-header from Missouri Western with a pair of fantastic seventh-inning rallies." "Fantastic," a breathless sort of word from a newspaper not immediately taken with the new program. Mr. Corbitt was completely blown away by Mike Davis's heroics. Davis, who "saved his fourth home run of the day—that's right, his fourth—until the Shockers were one out away from defeat in the nightcap." And there was one more sentence to suggest the delirium occasioned by the wins: "As dramatic as that comeback was, the first-game rally was even more incredible."

Believable or not, the wins were particularly significant, as they lifted the Shocks above .500 to an 11-9-1 record. Also of significance was the appearance in the Golden Griffons' lineup of several Wichita-area players who provided much of Missouri Western's firepower: Blake Schreck from Wichita South High School, Wes Schulz from Wichita North and Randy Parker from El Dorado, all of whom homered in the opening game. Mark Henrion from Wichita West, the starting pitcher in the opener, was staked to a big lead by his homies until control problems and successive big hits by Davis and Bob Bomerito sent him to the showers in the seventh. With this homegrown talent wearing the uniform of the visiting team, Coach Stephenson could take some cold comfort in the fact that in years to come, he'd get first look at any Division I prospects in Sedgwick and surrounding counties.

ANOTHER NEW COACH AND AN UNDERDOG

Oklahoma State University had suffered through a difficult 1977 season, winning just sixteen games while losing twenty-eight, an embarrassing .364 winning percentage. It was so embarrassing, in fact, that it warranted the firing of Coach Chet Bryan and the arrival of a new coach, Gary Ward. Coach Ward's influence was immediate and profound, as he would lead the Cowboys to forty wins on the season and to the championship of the Big Eight Conference Tournament. When the Shockers arrived in Stillwater for a double-header on April Fools' Day, they found an OSU team on a tear with a sterling 20-6 record.

OSU pounced fast, pounding out a 4–0 lead in the first two innings. And then the Shocks did a little pouncing of their own, loading the bases in the top of the third with two outs. Bob Bomerito then laced a single to center to score Kevin Akenson, as Phil Cordova hauled on around third in an attempt to score from second. But a perfect peg nailed Phil at the plate; rally killed. The Shocks would put together just two more runs in the first game of the twin bill, while the Cowboys continued the onslaught of twenty-nine hits on the day against four different WSU pitchers. Cowboys 12, Shocks 3.

The second game was called at 5:45 p.m. because of darkness, a decision made with some protest from the WSU bench because the Shocks were mounting a threat late in the game, scoring six runs total in the fourth, fifth and sixth innings. Who can say what a lingering sun might have meant to the outcome?

No excuses, though.

The Shocks enjoyed, at last, a non-game day on Monday, April 3, 1978—even Gene Stephenson might admit the need, every now and then, for a day not consumed by baseball. As it turns out, with Kansas State waiting, the rest may have been overdue, but it wasn't overly helpful.

Gene had spoken in the newspaper about Tuesday's double-header, calling them "our most important games to date." "We're definitely the underdogs, but the pressure's on them," he said publicly. "I really don't think K-State can afford to lose to a first-year team." Their 11-10 record notwithstanding, the Shockers looked almost unbeatable on paper—were offense the sole determinant of winning. The team's batting average was an absurd .346, an average third best in the nation, with one of the teams in front of them, Western Kentucky, having played just ten games. Seven of the eight regular Shocker batsmen brought with them an average in excess of .300. Two players were hitting in Ted Williams land: shortstop Mike Davis at a .436 mark and third baseman Bob Bomerito at .432. Mike also led the team in homers with nine, while Bob led in doubles, total bases and a hyper-productive forty-one RBIs. Gene offered a credible explanation for the team's prowess at the plate: "Our players worked hard in an extensive off-season weight-training program to go with their strong effort to perform as coached."

That said, Gene worried about his team's ability "to stay relaxed and not make too many mental mistakes like we did against Oklahoma State. We're starting to play better teams now, so we won't be able to keep having the mental lapses we've had in the past." Meanwhile, Wichita State pitchers had ballooned to a combined ERA of a blubbery 6.32, as opposing batters hit cleanly one time out of four. The smiling Stephenson said that he nonetheless expected game experience to improve the staff's record, especially as injured pitchers Mitch Denson and Chuck Linhardt returned to the rotation.

Wildcat pitching was to make a major contribution to K-State's sweeping both games, but a couple fat pitches from WSU hurlers may have given the Cats even more: a run-scoring double and a two-run homer among eleven K-State hits. Shocks lose, 7–2.

In the second game, Shocker starter Bob Burgess was rocking a 3–1 lead in the sixth, thanks to a two-run homer from outfielder Dave Howard and a K-State fielder's choice that brought in Bob Bomerito, who had doubled. And then the foolishness began. "What beat us was all our mistakes," Gene moaned. "Burgess should have had a shutout." Mistakes such as a fumbled double-play grounder rundown in the outfield followed by a wild throw, a throw into the K-State dugout as a matter of fact, and suddenly the eighth batter in the Wildcat lineup, a .146 hitter, had driven in the winning runs. Kansas State 4, Wichita State 3.

Down for the Slog

The Shockers then began a month of avoiding losses too humbling to imagine—barely beating little Friends University, for example, with its 1-7 record—and then rising to pound out umpteen hits in games called on the run rule after five innings. Then Creighton bused south from southeastern Nebraska, the Jesuit school ranking behind only Tulsa in the heat and force of Wichita State's rivalry. Were it not for better equipment, better opportunities to practice in cold weather, a better field, a couple restrooms and a press box and the other amenities associated with college athletics at the highest level—were it not for those slight differences—Creighton would have come to town in an overall condition not unlike WSU's: young, inexperienced and obviously operating more on excitement and raw talent rather than disciplined team play refined in a long-established collegiate baseball program.

The young Shocks walked into McAdams Park (one dollar for adults, fifty cents for kids) on Friday, April 7, having played thirty-two games in twenty-six days, grizzled veterans with their game faces on. The Shockers were doing their level best to ignore the highs and inevitable lows of their seasonal performance, trying instead—at their coach's strong suggestion—to work relentlessly on what they weren't doing well but to think now and then about what they might be doing better than most. Team hitting, for example. In the meantime, Gene Stephenson, across the way there in the front row of the McAdams grandstand, was penciling in his starting pitchers, both unbeaten: Matt Yeager in the first, Bruce Morrison in the second. Their fates could not have been more dissimilar.

In the day game, the Shockers began slow and finished slower still, giving up ten runs in the fifth and sixth innings alone. The Blue Jays entered the game batting a tepid .204, but they soon found their bats, including a grand slam home run by Creighton's sophomore catcher, who had batted exactly .000 theretofore. With nine walks surrendered by Matt Yeager and relievers Dave Waddell and Scott Bready, the final score, 15–7, was altogether predictable. And then Gene called a team meeting.

"We had a long talk between games," he said. "I was disappointed with our pitching and our hitting alike. We didn't fight the opposition. Our pitchers didn't challenge the hitters, and our hitters didn't challenge Creighton's pitchers. I hate to see that lack of fire. I really do hate it."

In the night game, the Shockers seemed to have listened, going into the bottom of the fifth leading 3–1. Evidently, Gene had a little something incendiary to say to the Shocks scheduled to bat next. WSU brought five runs across the plate in the fifth and six more in the sixth, the showpiece slug a grand slam from first baseman Larry Groves. Bruce Morrison pitched one of the best games of the year (losing his shutout to an unearned Creighton run), and enjoyed some stellar glove work behind him, Dave Howard showing off with a hard-charging, shoestring catch followed by a bullet to second to double up a Blue Jay runner. Final: WSU 14, Creighton 2.

It was the same team—at least the same guys wearing the same jerseys—as the first game. And thanks for the words of encouragement, Ten. Sunday's finale completed the seesaw movement of the Shocker season to date, as the pitching staff threw a bunch of strikes, good pitches that Creighton batters proceeded to cream all afternoon long. It was a mirror image of the game the evening before: Creighton 14, WSU 3.

Now the Missouri Tigers, fresh from a sweep of Bradley, waited down the interstate with a 17-10 record and big sticks of their own, some hitters swinging in the high .300s. It would be another long ride with not many happy thoughts en route, not much laughter at all, in the Shocker vans leaving Columbia after losing both games of a Sunday double-header by a combined score of 15–2, admittedly against a Missouri ball club that Coach Stephenson called "the best team we've played all season." So as the three vans crossed over the Kaw River back into Kansas, where a K-State team waited after two victories over WSU just the week before, Gene and his players took stock of their 19-17-1 record, thinking that maybe they were beating the teams that their pure athleticism suggested they should, thinking that the good teams win the close ones, that good pitching almost always beats good hitting and that no one could question their effort or discount the odds they'd faced. Maybe they thought that the old baseball clichés didn't apply to them, that their current slump could be ascribed to too much time cramped up in suburban moms' delivery vehicles. As they passed through Lawrence, maybe they saw the two flags flying from the towers of Fraser Hall atop Mount Oread, and they reminded themselves that the Jayhawks had just pounded the archrival Wildcats in four games over the weekend. Maybe they thought, "Hey, Coach is right. We have nothing to lose. Let's play ball."

And they did.

The Shocks blew into Manhattan, crossing the Kaw again, with their minds solely and squarely on baseball, the hard-edged, take-the-extra-base Stephenson brand of baseball. Here's the *Eagle*'s grab on the results: "The Wichita State University Shockers ripped Kansas State pitching for 31 hits and swept a double-header from the Wildcats, 10–5 and 16–6." Gene's take? "These were big, big wins for us. We beat an established Big Eight program on its home field. It's a big plus that we put it on 'em pretty good." All of a sudden, the Shockers were closing in on .500 against established Big Eight competitors.

The Shockers then settled into a series of games against smaller schools, displaying that frustrating unpredictability that had, unfortunately, already become their calling card. "Who's going to show up?" was the question of the hour. In some contests, the Shocks' big bats drove enough teammates across the plate to overcome passed balls and porous fielding; in other games, unearned runs, blown catches, poor throws and mental mistakes took an obvious toll on Gene Stephenson's thirty-something hair color. The improvements came almost imperceptibly, practice to practice, game to game, the Shocks' record of 28-25-1 an indicator of the ride. Shocker hitting remained as potent as ever. Banged beyond recognition, Shocker pitching was coming out of the ice packs, ninety-mile-per-hour fastballs heading toward the plate, a good many of them strikes. Gene Stephenson was beginning to understand full well the raw talent he had found, and that talent was turning into team play, every man on the squad practicing even harder now, believing now that they could hit, run, field and throw with any collegiate bunch in America.

"We'll see," Gene thought. "We'll just see."

THE MOST IMPROBABLY HAPPY
HEADLINE OF THE SEASON

WSU continued to split double-headers, failing to sweep obviously weaker teams. And then, one morning in May, the headline read, "Wichita State Whips OSU Twice." It was right there in undeniable seventy-two-point Times Roman, an implied assertion that the 1978 Shockers, just a couple of months into their rebirth, could play with anybody, as they beat perennial Big Eight contender (and eventual 1978 Big Eight champion) Oklahoma State in front of home folks who, maybe, were coming to believe. Gene had begun to talk to the newspapers more openly now, saying things such as, "We can do this every time out," referring to solid pitching backed by nationally ranked power hitting—the "this" that beat the 38-17 Cowboys, in strong contention for a berth in the College World Series.

A side note here, emblematic of the silliness surrounding the Shockers and their long-suffering attempts to find a place to play baseball. As Shocker Field opened for the last two games of the season, a scoreboard costing right at $100,000 flickered and firecrackered out next to Twenty-first Street as fans sat on truck beds and stood in line at Porta Potties. The poor scoreboard, misplaced and alone, seemed emblematic somehow of a season on the brink of greatness, its very existence an indication that not every promise made to Gene Stephenson had been kept, that not much thought had gone into the return of the baseball program over in the offices of the athletic administration. How might an electronic skyscraper (in Kansas's terms) come ahead of public restrooms and proper seating? Why would such an extravagance take precedence over bats and balls and the

In cold-weather baseball, fans must adjust to the rigors of sometimes-gray skies and brutal north winds. Eye on the ball, numb backsides.

occasional full-ride scholarship? Such questions lay for the moment beyond Gene's willingness, or ability, to answer. And so he turned his gunners loose: Larry Groves ripped a fastball over right-center at the 350-foot mark for the first home run in the new park. Bob Bomerito followed suit an inning later. Pinch hitter Tim Tolin smashed a grand slam, and suddenly everyone in attendance knew that the scoreboard might be big, it might be brightly lit, it might in its grandiosity be misplaced for the moment, but it absolutely could not display more than nine runs in one inning. With the ten-run rule suspended at the agreement of both WSU and Kansas Wesleyan, WSU's nineteen-run fifth-inning—a university record—drew everyone's attention to the board's inadequacies, both in terms of runs per inning and runs per game. "A hundred large and the damned thing can't count to twenty!"—or so the jokesters in the cheap seats might say, those seats at a dollar apiece still the best athletic value in town.

TOURNEY TIME

The 1978 Missouri Valley Baseball Tournament was played at Booth Field in Omaha, Nebraska, home park of the Valley's Creighton Blue Jays, with Wichita State slated to play Tulsa, the Hurricane winner of five of the six regular-season games between the two clubs. Randy Brown, the *Eagle*'s sports editor, echoed Coach Stephenson's assessment of the tournament and the Shockers' chances therein with his headline "Pitching Is the Key to WSU's Valley Title Chances." "All season long it's been two steps forward, one and a half steps back," Randy wrote. "The Shockers have been consistently inconsistent. The hitting has always been excellent. The fielding has always been shaky, although it has shone in spots in recent weeks. The pitching? Why even bother to go into it. But Stephenson's club also has proved that despite unpredictable defense and pitching, it can play against the big boys," with the team's six losses against Big Eight opponents coming earlier in the spring when "the Shockers were not nearly as good as they are now."

Booth Field was indeed small, particularly down the left-field line, where it backed up to Twenty-fourth Street in east-central Omaha, not far at all from the railroad tracks—or the snakes.

After batting practice, the pitchers in the bullpen were asked to retrieve home-run balls, no Rawlings to be lost. The poor pitchers found a steep, heavily wooded incline just outside Booth's left-field wall, home to rattlers and their offspring. With an already weakened pitching staff, the Shockers could ill afford a snakebite of any sort.

In the end, a half dozen homers blew out of Booth Field in the Shocks' 7–9 loss in the opener. On a single happy note, Gene noted that the bottom four hitters in his lineup accounted for each of the team's runs. Sadly, eleven Shockers were stranded on base.

The Shocks dodged the raindrops from a blackened sky and the line drives off some fully functioning Bradley bats in a game that the weather and the offense from both teams pushed to almost five hours—a twelve-inning, twenty-five-run knockdown, drag-out fight with the Braves that saw the Shocks, drenched but elated, hopscotch around the puddles to the dugout, a 13–12 victory in their muddied hip pockets.

The Shocker long ball asserted itself in another close game, this one a win against Indiana State that ensured Wichita State at least a third-place finish in the tournament—and continued contention for the All-Sports Championship of the MVC. The homers flew (no surprises in the team's ongoing big bats), but the real reassurance in the game came in the pitching performance of Bruce

Morrison, who threw a complete game, his nine innings pitched giving the bullpen another day to rest their arms after a 9–8 WSU victory.

And so it had come around to this: a couple games that might put Gene four years ahead of his prediction, a victory in the tournament sending WSU to the NCAA Midwest Regional, a thought that danced at the edge of his and his ballplayers' minds as the Shocks gutted it up for two the hard way. Tulsa looked, of course, for the Shocks to hit the ball well, but the Hurricanes could be forgiven a bit if they failed to anticipate the defensive pyrotechnics that awaited them. In a 3–2 squeaker, the Shockers relied on a six-hit, nine-strikeout pitching performance from a gutsy Larry Groves, who took advantage of some sterling mitt work from his teammates to escape jams in the seventh and eight innings, when the Shocks snatched away sure base hits, threw out runners at the plate and just generally owned the baseball. And suddenly, the team found itself in the championship game against—who else—the Salukis of Southern Illinois.

DOWN WITH DIGNITY

In printing that name again, the *Wichita Eagle* reported, "Groves himself led the nightcap explosion with four hits and four runs batted in, his big blow a three-run homer in the seventh." Groves saw his teammates claw back toward winning it all, with the tying runs on base in the ninth when "Saluki missile Dave Stieb struck out Dave Howard for the final out and the championship trophy." The legendary quality of the Shockers' first season in almost a decade suffered not at all in their championship loss, as they banged bats with a fully rested SIU in a 10–8 anybody's game.

In a way, it was fitting that the Shocks' last out of the season should come at the hands of an outfielder/relief pitcher who'd go on to win 176 games in the Majors, become a seven-time All-Star and throw the first no-hitter in Toronto Blue Jay history. Dave Howard saw only high hard ones, inside and then some, from Stieb, a flamethrower who led the National League in hit batsmen more times than young Mr. Howard's mom might care to count.

Chapter 3
THE PROMISED LAND IN SIGHT

In the days when he was still known officially as "James," Jim Thomas was a say-hey senior at Wichita Southeast High School, an All City League member of Southeast's 6A state-championship team who had batted a champagne .487 with an essentially flawless glove thrown in at shortstop. His new college coach admitted at the time that the premier edition of his Shockers' infield might have been "a little leaky." And Jim Thomas, the first player in Gene's '79 class to sign, was recruited as much for his fielding as for his timely hitting. Gene spoke of Jimmy's "strong potential," his "ability to be a great player someday" and the possibility of his "making our team as a freshman."

Thomas had been drafted in the fourteenth round of the MLB draft but soon decided to play collegiate ball. Recruited by Kansas, Kansas State and Missouri, among other big-time schools, Jim remembers, "None of those other schools were talking like Gene was. Right away, he's saying that we're going to Omaha…that we're going to be playing for a national championship. I thought to myself that this guy may be crazy, but I still like his thinking."

Other Shocker recruits were not so quick to pick, and especially since the Shockers' extended schedule had given Gene and newly arrived assistant coach Brent Kenmitz minimal time to scout and sign new players, a few anxious days passed in the early days of the summer of 1978. Gene had established "a successful recruiting year" as one of his three major first-year goals, the others being "winning half of our games" and "making significant progress toward the completion of our new Shocker stadium." Well, coach, two out of three ain't bad.

TEAM II

Gene scheduled his second annual Baseball Coaches Clinic for cold, early 1979, a confab featuring "Mr. College Baseball," Rod Dedeaux, head coach of the defending national champion Southern Cal Trojans. Jim Sundberg came from the Texas Rangers to talk with the high school and junior college coaches about the lonely art of catching, Jim routinely regarded as perhaps the best defensive catcher in the Majors at the time. Cardinal manager Vern Rapp had forced him to snip and shave in 1977, and now the reasonably well-groomed Al Hrabosky came to the WSU campus, his hair shorn, but his uncontrollable emotional tics still in place. A whack-job with a ninety-five-mile-per-hour fastball, "Mad Al" had won the *Sporting News'* designation as Fireman of the Year for 1975, when he led all National League relievers with twenty-two saves. Just as important to his invitation was the whole "I really, really don't like you right now!" mentality that Gene appreciated so much in a player. Major League All-Star and World Series hero Gene Tenace of the California Angels came to talk about hitting the ball with power, and he should know. Gene is the holder of the all-time World Series slugging record—an astounding .913—and the only player ever to hit home runs in his first two World Series at-bats. All in all, it was a roster of presenters that attested to the WSU program's immediate stature among the baseball community and to the obvious respect for Gene Stephenson within that group.

As the clinic closed, Coach Stephenson looked around at his gathered team and announced, "We'll be a contender," thinking of his new, stronger defense up the middle, where junior college transfer James Smith would take over at shortstop, allowing Mike Davis to return to his more comfortable spot at second. Third baseman Bob Bomerito was suffering from a mysterious arm ailment, but the multitalented freshman Thomas stood ready to man the hot corner. The outfield of 1978—Dave Howard (left), Kurt Bradbury (center) and Matt Yeager (right)—remained intact, with able backups in Tim Tolin, Keith Jones and Joe Carter, a largish freshman flanker from the WSU football team who had the "potential to be great," according to Gene.

Joe hadn't practiced with the team until January, after his football season had ended, and he, too, jogged up to the Hillside Y, where a single batting cage waited for the team—just as soon as they erected it again. Jim Thomas recalls, "Of course, we had all heard about this big-time football player, and here he was—a good athlete, a big guy—and he stepped into the cage and did not hit a ball. He really worked at his shortcomings, though. Joe was always happy. He was easygoing and steady…just had a great attitude. And not once did he ever big-league it on us. In his first weeks with the team, he was not a very good outfielder—not at all. He didn't throw exceptionally well, but he could run. And he was strong. Really strong."

And then there was the designated hitter, another big, strong guy with forearms and hands reminiscent of his coach's. Phil Stephenson had come up from Guthrie, Oklahoma, fifteen years Gene's junior, the kid brother who idolized the legendary hometown hero, the collegiate All-American, the military veteran, the young assistant coach with all the earned prerogatives at the university down the interstate. But when Phil, too, became a three-sport all-star in high school, the recruiters came calling, his brother noticeably absent. "I was reluctant to recruit him," Gene remembers. "It was a new program. I didn't want people to say, 'He's playing because he's a relative.'" Assistant Coach Terry Jolly thought otherwise. "You're crazy not to recruit Phil," Terry said at last. "He's the best hitter in Oklahoma."

Finally, in June, the phone call came. "I want to play for you if you want me," the big little brother said. And he arrived in Wichita and went to work. Phil remembers, "I had to come in here and really earn a job. I had to prove I could play—not just to my brother, but to everybody."

GAMES AND MORE GAMES

The 1979 Shocker baseball season grew even as it was being announced, swelling to ninety-three games in its final form, including home stands against Illinois, Big Eight power Oklahoma State, Iowa State, the cross-state rivals of basketball fury the Tulsa Golden Hurricane, Texas Tech of the Southwest Conference and, as advertised, "the biggies": two games against the University of Southern California. While the usual suspects in the national championship chase luxuriated in the California, Texas, Louisiana, Arizona and Florida sun, WSU had played more regular-season games than any other team in the country in 1978. As Gene announced the 1979 schedule, he mentioned in passing that he had arranged the games in such a way that his players would be missing only two days in the classroom; the sole extended road trip would come during spring break, with two other commutes scheduled during university holidays. In this regard, Athletic Director Ted Bredehoft added, "Gene's players carried more hours and earned higher grades in the spring semester than they had in the fall semester. Other schools might have more money, better

Jimmy Thomas would eventually become a coach at WSU, where he taught fierceness as the only way to play.

facilities, and a longer tradition, but nobody works harder than we do. We work all year round."

In those first years of the rejuvenated program, no NCAA rules impinged on competition; collegiate baseball teams might play as often as they wished. And Gene wished a bunch. "In the fall, we'd play junior colleges every day," Jim Thomas says. "We'd play in stages. The guys who got out of class early would start. Then the guys with early afternoon classes would come and play while the first group of players went to get something to eat. Crazy, crazy days."

The coach said of the schedule, "Nobody can say we took it easy. We aren't ducking anybody. We have asked to play some of the best."

PFFFFFTHOOOT

Wichita Eagle sports editor Randy Brown reserved "raspberries of a rancid nature" for Kansas State University and the University of Kansas for their refusal to come to Wichita to confront the Shockers. "Wouldn't you just know it?" was editor Brown's rhetorical question assigned to those long-established programs and their understandable fears about a team as explosive as the '78 Shocks had proven to be. There was nothing to be gained from risking a loss, maybe a hammering, from some no-name team without a proper field on which to play, some poverty-stricken upstarts with not a single outdoor practice before its season opener. "Stephenson now pronounces himself resigned to this kind of treatment from WSU's 'sister' institution," Brown wrote. "If Wichita State baseball continues to improve, KU and K-State ought to come begging Stephenson for games."

Randy Brown was just being realistic when, before his Pffffthooot at WSU's sister Kansas schools in Division I, he predicted "a long afternoon" for the Shockers as they traveled to Fayetteville to take on the powerhouse University of Arkansas for the season opener on February 25.

With injuries to key players—Bomerito and Groves chief among them—Gene told the gathered media that "'immediate help" would have to be forthcoming from the team's newcomers, newcomers such as pitcher Don Heinkel, who was scheduled as the "strong possibility," per Gene, to start the second game of the Razorback double-header. In fact, twenty-two of the twenty-five players on the Shocker squad were freshmen or sophomores, while Arkansas started six seniors and three juniors. "We're going down there to give it our best shot," Gene said. "But if we beat Arkansas, it could be the biggest miracle since the Immaculate Conception." A young and inexperienced team from the Missouri Valley Conference is just not supposed to be competitive with a mature and proven team from the mossy old Southwest Conference.

And then it snowed. It snowed a bunch in Fayetteville, Arkansas, and the double-header was postponed, with no makeup date set. But for the young and inexperienced team from the MVC, the trip did provide a genuine blessing: two solid outdoor workouts, including the Shocks' first full infield practice of the season.

Weather cancelled the first two games on the home schedule as well until at last, on Tuesday, March 6, the 1979 version of Gene's grand experiment took the field against the Falcons from West University Street on a dried-out Shocker Field. The team could not have performed better, sweeping the double-header from Friends 13–0 and 19–3. Of course, the thirty-two runs pounded across the plate were nothing new; the 1978 team had batted .351, averaging nine runs per game. The defense allowed just three runs in the two games, a stinginess that warmed the coach's heart, as his fielders played errorless ball.

More good news arrived off the field as well. Shocker Field was becoming populous with enthusiastic fans—so many, in fact, that they spawned one of the stranger headlines in *Wichita Eagle* history: "Athletic Director Looking for Spare Flatbeds." The headline was a reference to the additional seating required at future Shocker baseball games, the instant bleachers (a flatbed with risers) certainly needed for the big games ahead. Ted Bredehoft reported that he had acquired risers sufficient to the seating of another two hundred people, pending the arrival of two more trailers. Gene Stephenson reported, off the record, that an enthusiastic fan had fallen off the end of his bleacher seat, such was the crowding on the flatbed. "It's a sure sign of our success," Gene said.

The players, too, were optimistic, making the best of the logistics. "I thought our infield surface was the greatest in the world," Jim Thomas said.

As the flatbed-mounted, one-dollar bleacher seats began to fill, fans watched from along the first-base line.

"We all did. We didn't know any better, and besides, we'd been promised a new stadium."

Meanwhile, the baseball gods played stupid jokes on the Shockers. In a game against Southwestern scheduled for Flatbed Field, the university's radio station, KMUW, had strung cable, ready to broadcast the first game. But get this. The umpire crew declared the field "unusable" when, to quote the *Eagle*, "workmen painted the foul lines crooked." No facilities for folks with an overload of iced tea. Players changing clothes in their cars. *Eagle* sportswriters taking their notes longhand on their thighs. Fans scooching tight and tighter still on a precious few one-dollar bleacher seats. And now there were drunken line-drawers!

The horror persisted in a final slap at Shocker baseball's stature in terms of a place to play: the games, quickly moved to McAdams, were ordered to conclude by four o'clock when a local prep game was to be played. Get off the field, Wichita State University. Wichita East High School is here. As a matter of fact, many home games—such as they were—began at noon in the 1979 season to avoid these conflicts at McAdams or at West Side Athletic Field, where prepsters owned the diamonds outright.

No matter. The Shocks followed with lopsided wins over Kansas colleges Bethany and Tabor, mauling the smaller schools by a ridiculous 62–5 margin in the four double-headers.

Pfffffthooot no more.

Ass-Kissing at Second Base

March 11, 1979, proved geographically interesting as the Shocks managed to play two away games against two different schools at a single distant, non-tournament site. The logistics of the coming together of Wichita State, New Mexico State and the University of Denver in Las Cruces, New Mexico, on that late winter day do not matter now, but suffice it to say that the Ides of March were very kind indeed to WSU, as the team went undefeated for the week.

Eager to share the good news, Coach Stephenson was on the phone: "On the New Mexico trip, I'd call back to the newspapers, hoping to get our scores reported, only to discover that the beat writers were covering a basketball game. I then called Henry Leavitt Arena, hoping to talk to a reporter so the results could appear in the next morning's paper. In fact, I reached the alleged sports information director, who informed me that he didn't care what our scores might be. He just flat didn't want to know. So I call back, and this time I get the trainer for the basketball team, and he tells me that there's just no need to report our scores because 'nobody cares.' He goes on to say, 'If baseball ever makes a dime at WSU, I'll kiss your ass at second base.'"

THE FIRST LOSS, A CLUSTER OF WINS AND A REALITY CHECK

The season's first loss came courtesy of the Miners of the University of Texas–El Paso. So much for perfect seasons, as UTEP used timely hitting and the Shockers' propensity for leaving men on base to win the first game of the series 9–8, a heartbreaker for sure. The players had believed their coach when he told them that collegiate baseball was beginning to take notice of them, their monster batting averages, their extra bases taken. Big wins followed over teams that had plagued them a year before: Creighton, Texas Tech, Oklahoma State and Tulsa, with its home umpires. WSU beat Illinois and a bunch of smaller schools that came to Wichita afterward in the warmth of a baseball sun.

Baseball loves its twitches, its personal tics and public tantrums. Arguably, baseball engenders more mind games than any other sport. Few spectacles invite as much scrutiny as a once-solid ace struggling to find his stuff. No one on this planet of seven billion people is lonelier than an erstwhile slugger in the middle of a disastrous slump. And such suffering begets a fascination with the details surrounding baseball players' failures—and their successes as well. So did Gene and his young team pull out every trick in their collective book as defending national champion Southern California took the field on April 9, and a cold, lonely, occasionally dark night began for the Shockers and the curly headed gentleman in the third-base box, clapping his hands, rubbing his chest, tugging at his ears and searching—searching for a sign in the stands, any omen among the 4,011 fans filling Lawrence-Dumont Stadium to watch their upstart Shockers take on a legend.

And then the lights went out.

The electricity disappeared. And every superstition in the baseball book was insufficient to changing what happened next. After twenty-six minutes, the lights came back on, and Southern Cal commenced to pummel WSU

13–1. Any pitcher in Rod Dedeaux's bullpen seemed able to silence Shocker bats, bats that had theretofore been nearly unbeatable. For well more than two hundred minutes, the game showcased all that was best about a national champion—all that might have gone better for a second-year team in search of a spotlight. There were no mercies to be found that night, and even electricity could save the Shockers no longer. The frigid weather seemed to stiffen Shocker gloves as WSU handed USC three unearned runs in the first inning and two more in the fourth, five errors altogether. As always, Coach Dedeaux could not have been more gracious. "We had three freshmen hit home runs, and WSU made a couple of mistakes early. That's baseball. Tomorrow it could be the other way around."

Well, maybe. The Shocks started Matt Yeager, who had shone in his previous two starts, giving up just five hits in eighteen innings, a no-hitter stolen in his last outing. But Southern Cal's lineup was packed with big left-handed hitters, who watched Matt's right-handed motion all the way to the plate, where they stepped into the pitch, hitting tape-measure shots to right. Over the scoreboard in right. Over the scoreboard into a thirty-mile-per-hour wind in right.

USC head coach Rod Dedeaux recalls, "I brought my defending national champion University of Southern California team to Gene's campus to play a series of games at a date and in weather conditions that, out our way, we would have considered the dead of winter. Now that's respect."

"We were tight," Gene said. "We came out tight." And so it ended, the largest crowd ever to attend a college baseball game in Kansas having dwindled to a long-suffering few dozen. The lights flickered again, and any lingering thoughts of an upset disappeared into the dugout with Mike Davis after circling the bases alone, his home run in the seventh producing the sole WSU run.

"It was a terrible thing to happen—to all of us," Gene said with not a hint of apology. "All of our players are totally dejected. I feel especially bad for our sophomores, who have worked so hard for me in this program. I see so much talent on our team—it was just one of those nights." All in all, a series from purgatory, this Southern Cal deal, as a cold rain creased the city all day Tuesday. Gene begged his friend and colleague Rod Dedeaux to stick around an extra day, to play the second promised game. The coach looked into the night for a chance at redemption for the Shocks, one more shot at proving themselves on what might have been a national stage. "We tried till one o'clock in the morning to get them to stay for one more game, but they had trouble working out flight arrangements."

It was something new for the Shockers: an opponent that jetted to its away games, a team with frequent-flier miles versus the Shocks and their aching rumps and cramped-up thighs crawling from the drafty vans that hauled them around the great Southwest. Nonetheless, USC promised a return date in 1980, and Gene discussed the sheer spirituality of it all: "There is some mystique about playing Southern California, just like there is in playing UCLA in basketball or Oklahoma in football."

Something else was new, too. "We came out tight, and then we quit. I had never seen us quit," said Stephenson. Hateful, that word. Unused theretofore, foul-mouthed the sound.

LIFE AFTER THE UNIVERSITY OF SOUTHERN CALIFORNIA

The script from any baseball movie ever made called for the Shockers to storm back from their humiliation at Lawrence Stadium, biceps bulging now, eyes ablaze, strong jaws set, bats locked and loaded, as indeed the Shocks did with rampages over New Mexico State, 18–1 and 15–5. Third game of the NMS series now, runners on first and third, two outs in the last inning. The heroic Matt Yeager at bat. Long fly ball. Game over. Aggies 6, Shockers 5.

Now 38-9 on the season, a sparkling record by any accounting method, the team pounded out easy wins over lesser opponents, a long skein of successes highlighted by late April beat-downs of the Tulsa Golden Hurricane—9–0, 15–5, 18–4—and by hometown victories over the Razorbacks of Arkansas. Three weeks of perfect baseball with only a one-run loss to Oklahoma City had brought WSU's post-USC record to 23-2.

And then, in the last games of the regular season, Gene's guys confronted the Oklahoma State Cowboys in a strange home-away deal with four contests in two days, 128 miles apart. OSU won three out of four, the Shockers avoiding a sweep only by a 13–5 victory in the second game in Wichita. In the victory, Joe Carter launched a ball out of sight until it landed on the far side of Twenty-first Street, only to watch it called foul.

All in all, it was not a particularly auspicious segue to the valley tournament.

Fly Balls Hanging in the Springtime Sky

The MVC baseball tournament came to town for the first time from Friday, May 18, through Monday evening, May 20, 1979. The tournament came as had so many Wichita State baseball recruits: on the strong promise of a spectacular new field on which to play. The lack of facilities had little effect on the competitors, however, as the tournament began—as do almost all things Wichita—in the wind.

Wichita State, 64-13, set about some pre-tournament scouting, with a first-round bye on Saturday to play Tulsa on Sunday, winner over New Mexico State. The Shocks came out sluggish, as opposed to slugging, and then stayed sluggish. The 7–4 loss to Tulsa might have been predicted, this the Tulsa team the Shockers had beaten five times in a row, the least of these victories coming with a nine-run spread.

Also on Saturday afternoon, Indiana State, having abused Bradley on Friday, beat the nationally ranked Salukis of Southern Illinois 10–8, sending the defending conference champs into the losers' bracket with WSU—but not before the Shocks took their turn against the Braves. The newspaper account of the game accused Gene of "chortling." "'Not a bad performance against the wind,' chortled Shocker coach Gene Stephenson," we read. Wichita State 20, Bradley 6.

Next up: predatory Southern Illinois. A "runstorm," the headline called it, a "shellacking." Salukis 18, Shockers 3. "Everyone gets blown out, and it happened to us," Gene said, with all the matter-of-factness at his disposal.

And so the 1979 season ended, the Shockers taking home a 65-15 record, tying the 1976 Arizona State Sun Devils for most victories by an NCAA baseball team in a single season. NCAA tournament rules conspired to deprive the Missouri Valley of a second team in the tourney, a rule stipulating that only conference champions and runners-up can be invited to the dance. WSU, its sixty-five wins a non-factor, was automatically disqualified for its third-place finish, as the MVC tournament had no round-robin play to determine a conference champ.

Eagle editorialists railed against the rule, calling it antiquated and rude and wrong in so many ways. Well, two ways: "The rule is bad for two reasons. First, if there is a sport where anybody, absolutely anybody, can win a game or a short series, baseball is it. Almost every conference has a post-season tournament. The number one team in the country could come into its conference tournament, lose a couple and finish third. Or last. And second, why should a league be limited to two bids? If a conference has three or four or five teams of national caliber, why not invite them all? "

All that said, even the hometown newspaper admitted that "Wichita State probably didn't deserve a post-season bid. The Shockers played poorly late in the season and got worse in the valley tournament. They lost five of their last seven games."

A BRIEF SHOWER OF HEARTBREAK ON A SEA OF SUCCESS

Those games cast but a momentary shadow over a season of remarkable accomplishments, the disappointment of the MVC tournament giving way to recollection of hundreds of dollar-a-game thrills, the Shocks having sold one thousand season tickets in their second year back. While one thousand fans may not, from this distant vantage, seem like a particularly impressive number, it must be noted that only Arizona State sold more season tickets in 1979. Not Texas. Not Miami. Not Oklahoma. Not LSU. Not the University of Southern California. But WSU, with its fans' frozen derrieres parked on flatbed trailers. WSU, with no permanent restrooms. WSU, without lights. A program nonexistent just eighteen months previous attracted more season-ticket purchasers than all but one of the traditional

The 1979 Wichita State Shockers. *Bottom row, left to right*: Don Heinkel, Phil Stephenson, Mike Davis, Keith Jones, Jimmy Smith, Frank Pena, Jim Thomas and Phil Cordova. *Middle row, left to right*: Smokey McCarthy, Matt Yeager, Terry Hayes, Stan Brown, Walt Hagerty, Kurt Bradbury, Rob Burgess and Terry Williamson. *Top row, left to right*: assistant coach Terry Jolly, Chico Martin, Mitch Denson, Larry Groves, Bruce Morrison, Joe Carter, Chuck Linhardt, Tim Tolin, Dave Howard and graduate assistant coach Brent Kenmitz. Not pictured is head coach Gene Stephenson, who was out recruiting.

hothouses of collegiate baseball. And those WSU fans witnessed a show, all right.

With an outfield athletic and largely uninhibited, Keith Jones named the three of them "Earth, Wind, and Fire": Dave Howard, wild and free—"a handful," as Brent Kenmitz remembers him—was Fire; Keith himself, the fastest player on the team, was, of course, Wind; and Joe Carter, the strong, soothing and stabilizing influence on them both, was Earth. A workable metaphor here, accurate, applicable to the team as a whole: ballplayers in dynamic tension making the game plays because they had, over and over again, made the practice plays.

The 1979 Shockers established or tied eight NCAA team records: team batting average (.384), runs scored (828), RBIs (714), total bases (1,506), team slugging percentage (.625), doubles (181), most wins (65) and most extra-base hits (333). The records accumulated, making the untimely tournament slump all the more painful, baseball the most humbling of team sports, as the Shocks' coach was always reminding them. And the thoughts of what might have been lingered long after the bases had been stored away for the summer. Hadn't WSU beaten Big Eight champion Oklahoma State? Hadn't the Shockers pounded Texas Tech and Iowa State and Illinois and UNLV? Good gosh, hadn't they beaten Arkansas, the Razorbacks the eventual runner-up in the 1979 College World Series? Gene Stephenson and these young men with a common fire in their bellies had most certainly shown themselves to be three-dimensionally, substantially, unmistakably, real.

Phil Stephenson, Dave Howard and Joe Carter were chosen to play for Team USA in the post-season competition against Cuba, a bunch of collegiate all-stars that also included Terry Francona, the erstwhile manager of the Boston Red Sox who, way back then, had chosen the University of Arizona just ahead of WSU in Gene's first few weeks of recruitment. The team played well, finishing with a 5-3 record, but the genuine excitement came off the field, as the Cuban baseball faithful believed that the United States had sent the son of the president himself to play against them. Joe Carter, they reasoned, just had to be old Jimmah's kid, variable skin tones meaning nothing to fans in Castro's Cuba who, almost twenty years after the revolution, still did not have television.

Meanwhile, Gene was going north to Alaska to coach the Anchorage Glacier Pilots. It was the first time the National Baseball Congress team had ever found a coach east of the West Coast, a sure sign that amateur baseball was discovering what professional scouts already knew: some ball playing was going on in Wichita, Kansas.

Chapter 4
THE THINKING BEHIND THE PLAYING

Baseball, its believers would argue, operates with an essential purity, a deep-down freshness that keeps its adherents forever young. Other sports may change, may have to change, but baseball goes on forever.

Basketball may soon be requiring a higher goal, eleven feet or more if the professional version of the sport hopes to retain finesse and ball movement and defense as elements of the game even remotely as important as lob passes to waiting dunks. Football at its highest level of play necessitates the pass these days: the field is simply too small to accommodate the size and speed of defenders against the run. But baseball, at least in the fading light of an April evening, remains as it always has been. Little boys with mitts the size of their chests are playing catch across America, back and forth with their rubber-coated Rawlings, in the promise of a new season with new talent coming out of a farm system that doesn't ever have to end.

Coach Gene Stephenson begins to talk about *The Natural*, the movie starring Robert Redford as Roy Hobbs, the man who struck out Babe Ruth on three pitches, the man who cratered a fastball to explode the stadium lights and win a game he had been paid to throw to a gambling syndicate. At sixty-seven years of age now, Coach Gene Stephenson of Wichita State University would not be embarrassed for anyone to know that he's crying a little as he sees, in his mind's eye, old Roy step into that fateful pitch.

Maybe Gene has read Bernard Malamud's *The Natural*, the book on which Barry Levinson based his movie. Maybe Gene hasn't read the novel, which ends far differently than the orchestrated good feelings of the flick. The book concludes with two scenes: in the first, one villain loses his glass eye to a haymaker from a newly righteous Roy and another villain messes his pants after a Hobbs left jab, while Roy's ex–lady friend attempts suicide; in the second and final scene, Roy leaves the stadium, only to glimpse a newspaper stand screaming headlines that he threw the game, and when a newsboy pleads with him to denounce the charge, Hobbs breaks down and weeps. These are the details of life outside baseball.

Roy has truly left the stadium.

In Gene Stephenson's dampish eyes, the lessons of baseball have to be learned inside the lines, ninety feet to safety, ninety feet to surety in four directions. "Because baseball doesn't change, its lessons apply, no matter how much the world or the popular culture changes outside of baseball," he reasons, and the precepts of his fifty years' experience of the game come easily still.

"Practice doesn't make perfect. Practice makes permanent."

"You have to play hard every day."

"Enjoy the ride. It's the journey, not the destination."

"Love your teammates."

"Surround yourself with good people. Ignore the losers."

"Impossibilities are just opportunities waiting to happen."

"Work on the things you don't do well."

And on he'll go amplifying baseball's commandments, its gathered wisdom, with stories of players he has coached, of young men whose lives have been changed because they saw and then respected the evolved rightness of sixty feet, six inches between the rubber and the plate. Not an inch more or a foot less. Baseball has its unchanging rules and rubrics because only when players go by the book can there ever be the game.

And ain't it funny how the circle is a wheel?

WHY SOUTH CAROLINA WILL BEAT FLORIDA TWO GAMES OUT OF THREE

"Routine plays. South Carolina made the routine plays consistently," Gene says, speaking of the final game of the 2011 College World Series, wherein the Gamecocks won their second straight national championship. Gene says that a less talented team can beat the better athletes with preparation, "with practicing at game speed." Because he had thrown hard all year in practice, South Carolina's Michael Roth delivered eight innings of superb pitching in the deciding game of the series. He did it on three days' rest, as his teammates held Florida in firm control throughout the 5–2 win. "We're not the most talented team, and we don't have the best players, position for position," Roth said after the game. "But we go out and stick together as a team. We battle. I can't describe it. We're a bunch of average Joes, but we love each other, and we come out and we battle."

It's enough to make Gene Stephenson cry, this unselfish statement of fealty to the cause, of sticking together, of gutting it up to play every day. This is the means whereby a team wins sixteen straight NCAA tournament games, including eleven straight in the College World Series. But no, he's pumped now. No more tears as he talks of "fire in the gut," of the stuff that drove him to drag tarps from the football field to hang on the temporary chain-link fences lining the would-be baseball diamond at WSU, by himself in his earliest days, those tarps intended to persuade the few folks who came to the Shockers' first games to fork over a dollar to go and sit, all legal, in Gene's bleachers up on a trailer borrowed from Dave Stannard's construction company. Fire in the gut, all right. The self-motivation of his favorite players, the kids who came to him with a love of and respect for the game that led them to give not less than everything. Kids like he used to be, team captain at Missouri, hustling all the time, going hard, gutted up.

The Five Ds

The simple truths of the Stephenson approach to America's game have never changed. Over the years, that approach had distilled to what Gene calls the "Five Ds," a set of principles that, firmly held and frequently practiced, will lead to success every time, both on the diamond and in life.

1) Deserve It. "The players must believe that they deserve success," Coach says, but those right and just deservings come only to responsible people of accountable character, "young men who care about others." Early in their acquaintance, Gene asks his players a formidable question: "Do you like the person you've become?" Right between the eyes, that one. "Do you like the person you are?"

And then comes the rationale of the team concept, the basis of all that a group of players might become together. "Across all these years, no player has ever heard me utter the words 'my team,'" Gene says. "From the first day of practice, I urge these players to forget 'I' and 'me' and 'mine' and to think only in terms of 'we,' 'us' and 'ours.' Great team play simply cannot happen with selfishness from individual players." And then, in the shared responsibility and the shared reward of teamwork, comes a particularly good practice, the drills run just as their coach has insisted, every minute engaged with good people at game speed, every man with his game face on. And the thought comes—"Maybe we deserve to win a game or two."

Gratitude has its role to play, too. To whom much has been given, much will be required, the biblical injunction comes, and the coach steps again to the pulpit on the mound. "Usually, scholarship players' first trip back home comes at Thanksgiving," he says, "and I lean on the guys pretty hard. I tell them to hug their mommas, to walk up to their dads and say 'I love you' right out loud. Many of these parents have sacrificed a great deal in terms of their time and their money so that their sons could play baseball at this level, and they deserve to be thanked often and, as I say, out loud."

Gene doesn't push religion, not at all. But he does counsel his players to a deep spirituality, to faith in a Higher Power. "I tell them that there is a God, that their belief in Him will carry them through the tough times, that He has given them talent that they must use to the very best of their ability." He tells every one of his players to be the guy "who'll be there for his brothers. Because we'll win when we deserve to win."

2) Desire, the second of Gene's Ds, motivates from within, untaught (and probably unteachable). "A player has to want to win, to be the best he can be," the coach says, knowing that he can create only the environment in which personal desire translates to individual and collective achievement. "People have always told me how much they enjoy watching WSU play ball," the coach says. "Whether we're up by ten runs or down by ten, we play hard." As with those first players of his, the ragtag bunch of the early seasons, the secret waits in the wanting. The caps in the air and the piling on at home plate begins in the quiet yearning of a kid thinking that he loves this game, that he really, really wants to play this game.

The coach pauses for a moment, and he thinks of Eric Wedge. Eric Wedge, catcher on the 1989 national championship team, first-team collegiate All-American, Missouri Valley Conference Player of the Year, runner-up for the Rotary Smith Award for College Baseball Player of the Year, Major Leaguer with the Red Sox and the Rockies, American League Manager of the Year with the Cleveland Indians in 2007 and the current manager of the Seattle Mariners. That Eric Wedge. The year Eric won the AL managerial award, he wrote to his old coach, "I know now that passion and mental toughness are everything. Thanks for giving them to me."

Gene taught the joy that comes with hard work, humility, playing by the code and the love of one's teammates.

"I love Eric," his coach says, "but he's wrong. I didn't give Eric that passion, that desire to succeed, that willingness to do everything necessary to win. I just pointed it out to him. He simply flourished in the environment around here. The desire, the fire in the gut, that was all his."

3) Dream, of course, where obstacles float away and opportunities flash like signals from a third-base coach with arms forever moving. The great players dream. And they listen—to the small voices within them, to those old souls all around them who also believe that there isn't one thing in this world that is impossible. Never doubt. Never give up. Work hard. And harder still.

4) Discipline, self-discipline, which enables an athlete to work on what he doesn't do especially well. "It's fun to repeat over and over what you've

Joe Carter was not a baseball player when he came to WSU. His relentless work on his weaknesses made a natural athlete into a Major League hero.

already mastered," Gene says. "In life and in baseball, it becomes your responsibility to improve in every aspect of the task at hand, to pay close attention to the details of your work hour to hour." In time, an ethic of effort asserts itself, and the game gets played every day. Teammates watch each other work hard and harder still, and a trust begins to build, certain in the knowledge that when the call comes, they'll be ready. They will respond with discipline and confidence to the opportunities of the moment because they have practiced at game speed.

Joe Carter would not immediately come to mind as an exemplar of this sort of day-to-day grit. That would be unnecessary in Joe's case, right? The great Joe Carter—gifted in a way that few athletes could ever hope to be, right? Joe Carter, the five-time Major League all-star who went to the Big Leagues as the second pick in the 1981 draft, off to the Chicago Cubs after winning honors as College Player of the Year a few weeks earlier. That Joe Carter?

Joe grew up with ten brothers and sisters, most of them older, many of them as naturally athletic as he. All of Big Joe and Athelene Carter's kids were encouraged to follow their talents into whatever field of endeavor, athletic or otherwise. Little Joe played ball in the backyard, where a makeshift infield had been fashioned, where Big League announcers in his head called him to the plate, his natural athleticism already obvious to anyone paying attention.

By the days of his stardom at Oklahoma City's Millwood High School, Joe was a three-sport letterman: quarterback on the football team, forward on the basketball team and a pitcher on the baseball team. He did not go out for track, a conflict with his beloved baseball, but one spring day in 1978, he was sitting with some friends watching a regional track meet when the Millwood coach ran into the stands. The coach was wondering if Joe could broad jump, the team's regular long-jumper down with an injury. Joe changed clothes, walked to the pit, counted his steps and popped out there twenty-plus feet to win the event, which until that moment, he had never practiced. A week later, he won the state championship.

Joe Carter is now among the handful of the very best players ever to come out of WSU. Gene had been to Joe's high school as a football recruiter and had seen him play basketball. Gene recalls, "And when I told his dad that I was going to take this job at Wichita State, immediately he said, 'That's where my boy is going to play then.' And I told him, 'Big Joe, you better wait and see. I appreciate your confidence more than you can know, but you had better just wait and see.'"

God-given talents made Joe Carter a high school athletic phenomenon. Hard work and a prodigious discipline of self made him everything else. "The fact is, when he came here, Joe didn't know how to play baseball," Gene says with no hint of sarcasm. At eighteen years of age, the World Series hero hadn't yet begun to explore his baseball greatness. "Joe came to Wichita State, first of all, to play football as a wide-out and a punt returner. The deal was that he would be excused from football spring training to concentrate on baseball. And he went to work. He worked hard, especially in front of his teammates. He wasn't afraid to admit his weaknesses, to work on those aspects of the game in which, frankly, he had no experience. Remember, he was a pitcher in high school, and he played in only six games. Six! But Joe was hungry to learn." And so he humbled himself and set about correcting his mistakes in fielding and throwing and hitting and running the base paths with precision and modulated speed. He corrected those mistakes over and over in practice until he didn't make them anymore.

5) Dimension, the final D, is a sense of proportion in matters great and small, a humble understanding that no one is irreplaceable. "After the 1989 championship season, I had some occasional thoughts that maybe I was some pretty hot stuff," Gene admits. "People were telling all of us associated with the College World Series victory how much they admired us, how proud they were of our accomplishments. I'd be strutting around, full of

myself, and invariably a fan would come up to me and shake my hand and say, 'Hey, Coach Smithson! How's it going?' [mistaking Gene for look-alike Gene Smithson, the WSU basketball coach fired for multiple violations of NCAA regulations]. And I'd remember how important it is to laugh at yourself, to be humble and keep things in perspective."

To this day, that self-deprecation persists in Gene, who admits right out loud that, were he to disappear tomorrow, "this program would continue and not miss a beat." And the dimensional nature of things continues right up to all our disappearances, to the last question asked of any of us: "Did you leave the world a better place than when you came in?" The scorebook records the passage of the innings. The record book reports the accumulation of timeless achievements. But time will have its way, and an eternal sense of proportion asserts itself.

Gene Stephenson understands. "Baseball is a humbling game," he says. "And all that matters right now is the next pitch." Or, more importantly, the next practice.

AFTER ALL ELSE, RESPECT FOR THE GAME

Every true ballplayer understands "The Code," the unspoken, certainly unwritten notion of baseball as the best and only eternal game. It is the reverence for an innate fairness impossible, for example, in football, with its willful mayhem, the distinction between what's fair and what's finable coming in the angle of a helmet's injurious use, the fury of a nanosecond's onslaught. Baseball has rejected the instant replay with a righteous scoff, knowing that, in time, all will be made just and right. Witness Bob Gibson, the Cardinal's fireballing Hall of Famer, who waited fifteen years to settle the score with a batter who had shown him utter disrespect, Bob popping him hard in the shoulder with a fastball still capable of eighty miles per hour worth of hurt—in an Old Timers' Game!

And despite what the rest of the world might think of soccer, that sport borrows from baseball only its languid generality, its interspersals of intense, focused and crucial movement, bringing along none of the slow strategy, the thinking-man's genial input. Soccer has no slow, folded-arm discussions at the center of its field, no public decision-making on whose result hangs the entire game, these conferences on the mound governed even in their length by a gentle etiquette.

Coach Stephenson taught an aggressive style of baserunning. Come hard into the bag, but always spikes down—as per "The Code."

They float about, these unspoken rules, more moral than strategic. "Don't steal a base in a late inning with a big lead." Okay. "Don't walk between pitcher and catcher en route to the batter's box." Understood. "Don't talk about a no-hitter in progress." Makes sense. "Hitters, don't admire your home runs overmuch." Bad form. "Know when it's okay, even expected, to take out the catcher on a play at home." More subtlety creeping in now.

Playing at a level twice-removed from the Major Leagues, the Shockers of WSU's resurrected baseball program in a long-gone century's seventh decade were learning the intricacies of the game from a man who sheds an unashamed tear in baseball movies, who now and then uses *Tin Cup* as a coaching tool and who would have no truck with former Orioles manager Earl Weaver once telling Ross Grimsley, his weakening pitcher, "If you know how to cheat, now would be a good time to start."

Gene Stephenson was teaching these young men that baseball might be the ultimate means of shaping their attitudes toward one another, toward themselves. In quiet reverence of the game's traditions and its gentlemanliness, they might still play with intensity, with emotion unconcealed, displayed not in anger or intimidation but in motivation of oneself and one's teammates. Never show up an opponent, Stephenson taught, but hit hard, throw hard, run hard and, by all means, slide hard. Spikes down.

Chapter 5

GREAT FACILITIES, A WINNING TRADITION AND OTHER HALF-TRUTHS

Willie Mays, the Hall of Fame outfielder of the Giants and the Mets, headlined the third annual WSU Baseball Kickoff Banquet and Coaches Clinic. MLB's Player of the Decade for the 1960s was to speak at the leadoff banquet on Thursday, February 7, a twenty-five-dollar-per-person hullabaloo whose proceeds would support the Shocker baseball program and allegedly help complete construction on Shocker Field. Sponsors were being sought for Shocker players and bat girls to attend the event in the Hilton Inn's South Center Ballroom, the baseball program always with a hand out, it seemed. And it was necessarily so, with recognition from the university or its athletic department a sometimes halfway offering of no real certainty.

Willie was also to speak at the coaches' clinic, joining Kansas City Royals standouts Darrell Porter, Dennis Leonard and Frank White and 1979 National League Rookie of the Year Rick Sutcliffe, the Los Angeles Dodger who shared the mound with New York Yankee Ralph Terry, both showing their stuff for coaches to pass along to their youngsters. Opening Day was just over a week away, and the 1980 WSU baseball Shockers were going to learn at the knee of a twenty-time All-Star.

How unlike George Eugene Stephenson to qualify, but qualify he did as he looked out over his team in the last indoor practices, such as they were, before the opening of the 1980 season. "I think we'll have a better team this season," said Coach Stephenson, "but our record may not be as good for the simple reason that we play a much tougher schedule." Front-loaded that schedule, with big games early against the University of Hawaii and UNLV, warm-weather teams that practiced and played year-round in warm desert or tropical sun.

But Gene could look out over his guys, running again today the tightly scheduled drills that constituted their every practice. The short take on the '80 team as the season loomed.

Hitting: good team speed, reliable power, genuine problems for opposing pitchers up and down the lineup, always nine men in the lineup who can hit the ball out of the park, must guard against complacency based on 1979 performance.

Pitching: obviously the most experienced mound staff of the Stephenson era, to be made stronger still with the strong arms of left-handed freshmen; to Gene's mind the principal determinant of "how far we can go," this mound staff—"if they're consistent, we can be an outstanding team.

Defense: an entire infield returning, with a coach's expressed confidence in his outfielders, the experience obvious, the consistency to be determined.

In the matter of those astounding statistics of the Shockers at the plate, much of the credit must go to assistant coach Terry Jolly, who came with Gene in the first season. His boss called him "the finest man I've ever met in coaching." And those statistics, individual and team records, would have doubtless been much higher had Phil Stephenson been in the lineup as he deserved. "I was so hard on him last year," Gene admitted. "He should have started consistently as a freshman. A lot of times I started players ahead of him who weren't as good." This was the price the Stephensons paid to be together as Shockers, the brothers actually spending less time together than they had with Phil in high school, Gene seldom inviting his bro "over to the house. But Phil understood that from the start. We talked about it. He knew I expected more of him because he's family. But he made it a lot easier—he accepted the treatment even when I wasn't being fair." And on down the road, with Phil long gone, drafted into the organization of the Oakland A's, Gene would draw a long breath and say, "Those four years were the greatest thing that ever happened to me."

FRIGIDITY

Old Mathewson Junior High School had been shut down as a public school for ten years, a victim of the racial integration battles of the late 1960s, and the Wichita public school system had graciously allowed the Shockers to

74

use Mathewson's gym as an indoor practice facility beginning on January 14. But the lights refused to come on at the tiny gym at Eighteenth and Chautauqua Streets just west of the WSU campus. So for ten days, Gene's guys took to Henry Levitt Arena and its grudging welcome, foraging for cold-weather practice time among the castaway hours left over from the men's and women's basketball teams, WSU faculty on their noontime jogs and anyone else who might care to stake prior claim on the arena. So the Shocks lifted weights and played pepper in the tunnel and catch on the circular track at the concourse level and, in rare and happy and unprecedented moments, on the floor of the arena itself.

The lack of practice of any kind, and of the outdoor variety in particular, hurt the Shockers, who, per their coach, "have ability. Everybody knows that. But we don't look very good at all, and that's an understatement." With eight games scheduled against national powers on the opening road trip, Coach Stephenson announced himself prospectively happy were the Shockers to "come back home with a record close to .500." He had purposely scheduled the early going to be something of a wood shredder, knowing that if his squad played hard through the big names on the schedule, they'd be prepped for a run at Omaha as the month of May rolled around.

Meanwhile, somebody replaced some light bulbs in Mathewson Junior High School Gymnasium, and the team moved back in for a few days of practice (sort of) before the van ride to Fayetteville. "Man, it's tiny," Gene said for the record. "It's tough to even throw in here. But it's better than nothing at all, and that's exactly what we'd have if we went back to Wichita State University." Any casual listener detecting a barb in the coach's last sentence would have been entirely accurate in that detection.

Nebraska was to have come to town for a three-game series, even as the rains began, and Cornhusker officials spoke early of their concerns about the weather, thinking with which Gene concurred completely. The decision was made early that "we're not going to let them come down here unless there's a good chance we can play. Travel is too expensive." And he held out for the possibility of a double-header on Monday, March 1, the Shocks locked in and ready to play, having practiced outdoors for the first time in the week preceding. But Nebraska backed out. The field was dry, but temperatures in the high forties were apparently too much for the poor Huskers, who declined to play at the last minute. WSU, forced to settle for an intra-squad game, was happy just to be catching fly balls under a real, high, if clouded, sky.

And so the suddenly cosmopolitan Shockers were off to the fiftieth state on a shoestring budget without a game under their belts. Hawaii, meanwhile, stood at 13-1, including five wins in six games against Arizona State. *Collegiate Baseball* gave the team a little travel memento with the magazine's announcement that the Shocks were ranked twenty-second in the first NCAA poll of the season. Coach Stephenson scowled a bit as he read that Stanford—unbeaten Stanford—was ranked first in the country, its 12-0 record turning some polling heads despite the fact that every single one of those wins came at the expense of an NAIA team, Gene still sensitive to misplaced criticism of his scheduling and the gaudy records accomplished therein.

PLAY BALL!

Twice delayed but not shy at all in their first real competition, the Shocks swept the at-last-season-opening double-header against the University of Hawaii–Hilo, 8–2 and 13–6. The increasingly great Joe Carter showed the way, homering in his first at-bat of the season and following a few innings later with a three-run triple. Smokey McCarthy won the second game with late inning assistance from Chuck Linhardt and timely run support from Carter, who hit his second home run of the season, and Mike Davis, who hit his first and contributed four RBIs to the cause. Hilo dropped to 14-12 on the season, having played a ridiculous twenty-four more games than the suddenly sunburned Kansas kids who routed them.

Early in the morning on Sunday, March 9, 1980, the Shockers were again playing baseball against the University of Hawaii–Hilo, but this time the mainlanders watched an early lead slip away. In the top of the ninth, with the score tied 5–5, WSU had the bases loaded and nobody out. Then a momentary monsoon roared over the field, and as the deluge continued, the umpire stopped the game. With the majority of the grounds crew trying nothing more than to keep themselves dry, the Shockers ran over and jerked the tarp from the hands of the two or three groundskeepers attempting to do something useful, and the visiting team helped cover the field. Soaked but typically exuberant, the Shocks waited out the rain, which, when it soon stopped, would have indicated the resumption of the national pastime in this part of the world. The umpire, however, made a fairly large show of marching to the mound, looking around from that eminence and calling the game. He called the game—a 5–5 tie—without once peeking under the tarp to see that, thanks to the hardworking visitors, the dust of the base paths had barely been settled. Gene's erstwhile tarp-haulers were having none of this nonsense, and as one invading horde, they rushed the mound. The argument was on—eighteen to one, as a matter of fact—as Gene took the Hilo coach aside to talk reason with the man. Noticing the impending homicide back at the mound, Gene dropped all discussion, ran over and commenced to shove his players to the clubhouse, where, once inside, he locked them in. "They were that mad," he said afterward. "I honestly felt the need to lock them up." So Gene resumed his conversation with the Hilo coach, who agreed to finish the game.

After the players returned and limbered their dampish limbs, three Shocks reoccupied the bases. Joe Carter then came to the plate, but just as the Hilo pitcher went into his windup, the Hilo coach rushed to home plate for more high-level talk with the ump. Soon enough, the umpire raised his hand and called the game for the second time. Now it was Gene's turn to rush home plate, where he was told that the Hilo coach was worried that one of his players "might slip and be hurt." Slip and be hurt? In Division I collegiate baseball on an eighty-degree, if humid, Sunday morning? There was nothing to be done, Hilo having taken hometown rules to a new level of hometown fraud.

But wait. It turns out the Shockers should have been content with their ludicrous, un-American tie. Later that day, Gene picked up a copy of the *Honolulu Star-Advertiser*, in which he learned that his team had just lost to Hilo in a 5–4 squeaker, the newspaper content to report the score as received from, among the suspects, the Hilo sports information director or that pimp of an umpire. So, unless one chooses to believe the *Advertiser*, the Shockers record stood at 3-0-1.

A Digression upon "The Code"

The Shockers, in their sudden invasion of the umpire's personal space in the last Hilo game debacle, were, as their coaches quickly discovered, united. Every last player on the bench was either on the mound or en route to it—per "The Code." The *Star-Advertiser* undoubtedly used the pat descriptor "bench-clearing brawl" in its account of the proceedings, since in the Shocker scheme of things under head coach Gene Stephenson, per baseball's code, "If one of us comes out of the dugout, you may expect the rest of us sooner rather than later." Three years into the program's return to campus, the Shocks had traveled halfway around the world for their first-ever bench-clearing brawl.

And Stephenson's locking his players in the locker room represented a theretofore unheard-of concession to public safety, a Major League move in its implication of what to do per the unwritten rules. With Kansas guys confined to their temporary quarters, simmering there in relative humidity and absolute sweat, their coach had put the 1980 Wichita State University Shockers up there with what would be the biggest and best of baseball disagreements.

Meanwhile, Back in Paradise

"Shockers Hit Depths, Heights in Double-Header," read the March 12 headline in the *Eagle*, and give the paper props for accuracy. Rightly called "the most dramatic turnaround in the Shockers' young baseball program," WSU went from what Gene called "the worst performance since we restarted the program" to a sparkling 6–2 victory over the University of Hawaii–Honolulu.

The depths first: Murray State winning 2–1 in extra innings as a pop fly dropped untouched between two WSU infielders playing, per their coach, "way, way out of position." And so Stephenson gathered his thoughts and began the post-game conversation, no, the post-game monologue, no the post-game excoriation, with a warning: "I told the guys I was about to lose my temper." And lose it he did—to such a degree that in those intentionally hurtful moments, the Shocks transformed themselves. Terry Hays scattered four measly Rainbow hits while striking out eleven and was buoyed by a balanced offense, six different players driving in a run. Tim Tolin stroked his batting average to an even .500, same as Joe Carter's. The team as a whole was now at .330, down some from the atmospherics of '79. Their coach having chewed and spat out their backsides, the always fleet-footed Shockers picked it up a step and stole four bases. "You have to have speed to win here," explained their coach. "The wind is brutal...blowing in from left field. It's a big park. And it rains here."

Sometimes it rains on Hawaii's beaches, too, but the team managed to have some fun off the field. "They're having a good time everywhere but on the diamond," he said, his overstatement barely audible over the crash of Waikiki surf and the music coming from Don Ho's tree-top nightclub. The team was staying in "a fleabag hotel," the coach noted, "but we're going to take it to them [the Rainbows]."

Indeed, the Shockers did take it to them, the team returning to the mainland having taken three of four from the sixth-ranked Rainbows (although the weeklong visit ended sourly with a 7–3 loss on Thursday night). Gene boarded the plane with the considered opinion that if the University of Hawaii deserved to be ranked as the sixth best collegiate team in America, then Wichita State University deserved to be ranked fifth. As a matter of fact, Hawaii went on to play in the championship final of the College World Series in 1980, having lost only one series the entire year, that to the Shockers of Wichita State University.

The Shockers landed in Las Vegas on their way home from Hawaii, and in the course of seven hours, they scored thirty-four runs on thirty-seven hits to take both games of a double-header against Wyoming. When the last Shocker crossed home plate against the Cowboys, the team's batting average stood at .316, with a slugging percentage of .449. Warmed up and again ready for nationally prominent competition, the Shockers lost to ninth-ranked UNLV 5–2, the score in the bottom of the seventh when the umpire

The 1980 team boasted four hitters batting above a stratospheric .400. *Left to right*: Phil Stephenson, Bruce Morrison, Bob Bomerito and Joe Carter.

threw up his hands, declared it too dark to play and gave the home team the abortive win. The Running Rebels abruptly cancelled the next day's game.

In a scheduling scenario that can be termed only "lose-lose," the Shockers came off their high-powered, long-distance road adventure to play the teams available at the time. They drove down to Enid, Oklahoma, to placate Phillips University 13–1. Then they went back home to smack around the University of Minnesota–Morris, a team thrilled to be playing in relatively balmy late March Kansas for the Shockers' home opener. And Joe Carter was not about to disappoint the fans who had been waiting all winter for Gene's trailer-based bleachers. The big guy went four for eight in the two games, both easy victories (12–0 and 12–3). Then the rains came, forcing the postponement of the Kearney State game. And as the Shockers practiced indoors for nine days in anticipation of a pair of double-headers against Augustana College, the Vikings escaping frozen Sioux Falls to play in short sleeves on the last day of March, their opponents ranked fourteenth in the country on the day of their arrival in Kansas's largest city.

On the morning of March 31, Gene reported early to Shocker Field, as he always did on game days, to find a lock broken on the main gate. Further investigation revealed that April Fools pranksters had done their dirty deeds two days early. They stole the bases. Literally, in a non-baseball, criminal sense, they stole the bases. The pile of beer cans littering the pitcher's mound suggested the root cause of the theft, the empty Coors containers explaining perhaps the complete absence of logic in the crime. Semi-permanent, anchored in pipe set in concrete, the bases were manufactured with the male half of the pipe attached, essentially irremovable. They were not easily used and impossible to hock—immediately identifiable in any local dorm room. The absurdity of the loss bothered Gene to no end, and he was visibly angry in his morning-long pursuit of replacement bases.

The coach's irritation spread to his players as they vented their frustrations on Augustana pitching, exploding for an obnoxious fifty-three runs in the first two games. WSU won 28–4 and 25–1 that afternoon, those new bases stomped with regularity by Shocks en route to home plate.

Little Augustana College, the nice Lutheran school from South Dakota, found some relief on April Fools' Day itself, losing both halves of a double-header by a combined score of 33–6, much more reasonable than the games previous. The newspaper truthfully reported the coach's odd response to the Augustana games: "We were sort of dead." Dead? Eighty-six runs in two days, dead? The beered-up larceny was obviously still rattling around in Gene Stephenson's head somehow. Dead? His brother hitting his fifth and sixth home runs of the season to take the team lead in that category and what should have been Phil's seventh bouncing off the tip of the right-field fence for a double. Dead? Bob Bomerito going six for seven in the last game with six ribbies. That sort of dead?

Set for a six-game series in Wichita, the University of Illinois flew into town with a losing record, but all of those defeats had come at the hands of the Cowboys of Oklahoma State, then ranked sixth in the country. The number of runs dropped, and the margin of victory narrowed, but the Shockers came away with 8–5 and 7–6 wins in the first double-header against the Illini, games that were punctuated by a Bob Bomerito/Joe Carter double-steal, another home run from Phil Stephenson, four runs batted in from Jim Thomas in the second game, strong pitching by Terry Hayes in the first and the emergence of newcomer Don McGregor as a force at the plate.

Game Three went to the Shockers as well, 12–8, with homers from Mike Davis and Jim Thomas, his first. WSU's ten-game winning streak came to a sudden stop in the second game of April 4, as Illinois hitters made the best use of their eight singles to score seven runs. The Shocks' sole run came unearned. The Shockers again—this time for real—seemed sort of…well, dead.

It was another split the next day, as WSU resurrected itself to win 15–1 in the first game only to see Illinois jump to an eleven-run lead, against which the Shockers began to chip, that lazy old sun sliding down over west Wichita. With the score at 12–7 Illinois, the umpires called the game because of darkness, a sad fact not lost on the home fans, the double-header starting a full hour later than scheduled. And why? Because the umpiring crew arrived a full hour late.

And so it goes.

RAINBOWS IN THE COLD

The University of Hawaii took its early season losses to upstart Wichita State University with something like motivation, losing only once—to Missouri—in the interim, using pitching and team speed to full effect. Ranked fifteenth in the nation, one spot behind their congenial hosts, the Rainbows had just swept UTEP, and "they whipped the daylights out of Arizona State," this the assessment of the opposing coach. Meanwhile, "we played pretty horribly against Illinois," Gene reported. "I think our performance had much to do with the nine days we were forced to practice indoors. We aren't as sharp now as we were a month ago."

Nor were the Shockers sharp on those April 1980 afternoons in the ballpark on the banks of the Arkansas River, Lawrence-Dumont Stadium, the site of WSU's undoing at the hands of vengeful Hawaiians, who won 9–1 and 12–6 on their road to runner-up in the College World Series.

The Shocks rebounded with strong outings against New Mexico State and Northeast Missouri State, the Bulldogs enjoying a double-header with Wichita State in a combined score of 34–6 in favor of a team willing to say that, yes, we probably were looking past you to some big boys from the desert.

Coach Stephenson called it as he saw it: "We need to win this series because it will be a true indicator of our progress, the status of our program." With the fifth-ranked Running Rebels of the University of Nevada–Las Vegas arriving on a "hot streak," according to Coach Fred Dallimore, his team having won nineteen games in a row, the Shockers needed to play their best. Certainly better than their opening-game shenanigans when, in front of 233 flash-frozen fans, the Shocks found themselves burned 14–5, victims of a batting onslaught not unlike their own methods of run production.

Still, the sun rose the next day, warming Shocker spirits, Shocker bats and Shocker arms—Don Heinkel's Shocker arm most of all, the dreariness of the defeat the night before forgotten in the swings-and-misses of Don's masterful six-hitter. With his typical nonchalance, the pre-med major failed to understand the whoops, hollers and backslaps following his last pitch. "I forgot they had the win streak," he remembered.

A few hours later, the Shocks took the field again to play the Rebels under the lights at Lawrence-Dumont Stadium, where they proved beyond any doubt that they deserved to stand in the first rank of collegiate baseball teams. The Shockers won 10–6, with one last game to determine the outcome of the most important series of a substantial season.

Game Four brought sunshine on a Sunday afternoon on the WSU campus, some fans watching for free out on Pikers' Peak as they deepened their tans, the berm just past center field an ideal place for all sorts of fun on a budget. Ten spheroids falling at thirty-two feet per second would land among the sunning student bodies, as both teams hit the ball long, with five homers apiece. UNLV won the game 14–9, hitting its homers with men on base, many of them there courtesy of the ten walks issued by WSU pitchers. Meanwhile, the Shocks were content with solo shots until the ninth inning, when—too little, too late—they scored four of their runs. However,

Saturday's sweep of one of the top five teams in the country had already proven their worthiness. The Shockers belonged.

The Wichita State faithful, students of the game every one, received one of their most bitter, long-standing rivals with something like grace on the afternoon of Monday, April 20. In those games, poor Gene Shell and his now-homeless Tulsa Hurricane performed like a bunch of men who had recently been slapped hard and shown the door by women they loved. There's nothing like the elimination of the entire baseball program to take the edge off a team's competitive intent: the week previous, Tulsa University administrators had announced without warning that because of rising costs, of course, baseball would no longer be a varsity sport. The sub-story, unsaid at the press conference and winked at in the reporting, revolved around the federally enforced addition of varsity women's sports.

Promptly, as they say, Coach Shell had resigned. The man was just unwilling to watch his salary be cut in half, down to—irony of ironies—the pay at which his counterpart over there in the other would-be dugout had begun the Wichita State program just three years earlier. Ten-large, it seems, in this case was a figure of some dispute. "We just don't have anything to play for," an obviously dejected Shell said after the games, as the score indicated, the Shocks winning 13–10 and 12–6 in the twilight double-header.

The Razorbacks of Arkansas bused into Wichita on a roll, having just beaten on their home fields the third-ranked OSU Cowboys and the sixteenth-ranked Oral Roberts Golden Eagles, Arkansas showing off its own national ranking with something of a strut. Sad for the Hogs that their bus route brought them to town for one of the young WSU program's finest moments. The season's largest crowd gathered butt to butt on those bleachers, a record 604 fans losing feeling in their backsides while their Shockers embarrassed the visitors 6–2 and then an impossible 14–0. "This ought to put down all the dissenters who say we can't beat a good team," Gene suggested. "All we have to do is find some good clubs to play us," he said, the fullness of his opinion understandable in the heat of what his team had just done. It must be remembered that these Razorbacks went just ten months previous to the title game of the College World Series, losing there in a squeaker to Cal State–Fullerton. Back on the bus for the ride home to Fayetteville, the Razorbacks may be forgiven for their post-traumatic stress, this pounding at the hands of the unheard-of a bummer for sure.

A TOURNAMENT CHAMPIONSHIP AND ITS PUNISHMENT

Wichita State showed itself as the obvious favorite of the 1980 Missouri Valley Tournament, what with the best record, the highest national ranking, the best team batting average, the lowest ERA and a base-stealing success rate of 93 percent with 169 bags taken in 182 attempts. Also, the Shocks had ignited in the late going, coming into the double-elimination MVC event having found a way to win twenty-one of its final twenty-two games, that thorny loss to the disappearing Tulsa Hurricane still smarting as Gene turned his attention to the next five days in May.

And during those five days, the Shocks won four straight games: 12–3 over Creighton, 7–4 over Indiana State, 18–17 in a five-hour squeaker over Bradley and then 12–1 over Southern Illinois in the championship contest.

Immediately following the Shockers' shellacking of the Southern Illinois Salukis, the pretzel logic of the NCAA Baseball Tournament Selection Committee was made known in regional pairings that made always little and sometimes no sense whatsoever, two brackets in particular, the far Northeast Regional and the Midwest Regional, toward which the MVC Champion Shockers were, so much against their coach's will, directed. In their infinite, conniving wisdom, the committee stung trip wires all along the Shocks' path to the College World Series, the road to Omaha looped south through Tulsa, where waited Oral Roberts, Big Eight champion Missouri, Nevada–Las Vegas, Texas and the University of California—six teams of large caliber, demonstrated national powers.

Gene's disgruntlement arose from the pregame information that, had the Shockers lost to SIU, they would have been given an at-large bid to the Northeast Regional, where they would have confronted the historical baseball wherewithal of, for instance, Harvard—long-armed, big-boned studs with surgical sorts of hand-eye coordination up against what? Intellectual Puritans? Or the University of Maine. Or St. John's. Or East Carolina. Any one of these teams would have been simply unable to place in the top half of the Big Eight, Southwest, Pac-10 or Missouri Valley Conferences. Harvard versus UNLV? Come on!

In that unabashed way of his, Gene talked of forfeiture. He said right out loud, "If we didn't have so much pride, we were going to forfeit both games today [intentionally losing the double-header required for the Salukis to eliminate the theretofore undefeated Shockers]. We feel like we could go up to Maine and wipe that thing out. The NCAA has put maybe five of the top thirteen teams in the same regional. You figure that

The final out in the championship game of the 1980 Missouri Valley Tournament brought the Shockers into full celebratory mode.

out for justice." Silent for a second or two, Gene remembered that the Midwest Regional would involve six teams while every other site would host only four. His chest not entirely cleared, he continued, "If they want six teams in a regional, why didn't they get six in the Northeast? Then they might get someone who could play. If the NCAA is so intent on bringing the eight best teams in America to the College World Series, why the Northeast Regional? Why the Mideast Regional? They don't have a ranked team in either of them."

Coach Stephenson had been careful to keep his frustrations from his players. Knowing that the team was going to a regional, no matter the outcome of Tuesday's game against the Salukis, he turned his guys loose. "There was no point in telling the team. We wanted to beat the best, and we did." Jim Thomas remembers thinking that "there were big names in that regional—Arkansas, Cal, Oral Roberts—and, of course, none of us had ever been to a big tournament like that. We wondered if we belonged."

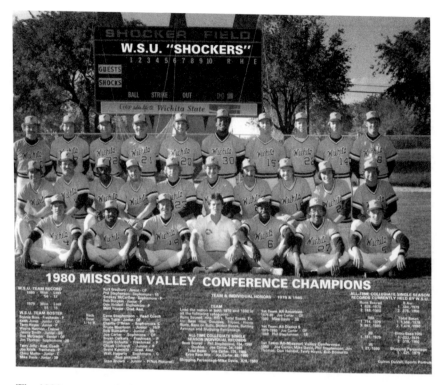

The 1980 team won the Missouri Valley Championship just three years into the return of baseball at Wichita State.

QUIETLY INTO THAT GOOD NIGHT

Big Eight champion Missouri came down to Tulsa with a 43-13 record, in a hitting slump of sorts, without a home run in sixteen games. Funny the turns a baseball team, a baseball player, a baseball game can take: the Tigers' light-hitting catcher, who had but three home runs all season, stroked a Joe Carter-esque shot more than four hundred feet into straightaway centerfield to break a 4–4 tie in the sixth inning, that solo round-tripper sufficient to give Mizzou the game.

The University of California–Berkeley's defense had carried the team into the Midwest Regional but betrayed the offense in the first-round game against UNLV when the infield committed atypical errors and the pitching staff failed to find its stuff. The afternoon of May 23 found the Shockers' defense porous, giving up easy runs, Cal needing just eight hits to walk away with a 5–1 victory that ended the Shocker season with a whimper. For their part, the Golden Bears then went on to win the regional.

Chapter 6
HEY, NEBRASKA

The most echoed word in Sedgwick County, Kansas, in the spring of 1981 was "Omaha." Omaha. Omaha, Nebraska, home of the College World Series, the all-but-certain destination of the Wichita State University baseball team, loaded as it was with Major-Leaguers-in-waiting, more talent with a bat than most teams would see in a decade, a bunch of guys who batted a collective .378 in the 1980 season, a time in which no one on the team—apart from a reserve catcher—failed to hit .300, a rock-solid .303 the lowest average for any of the Shocks. Four starters batted better than .400, a sparkling .331 the bottom bat number for the eight most-often-used players.

Of course, their coach was worried. Against his better judgment, he mouthed off to the newspaper, "I have to be optimistic. We return virtually everybody. But I do have concerns." Concerns that stood on the pitcher's mound, where the coach fretted about the toll the early season might take on Shocker arms, too many innings going too early to 1980's most-used hurlers, Don Heinkel and Terry Hayes. Meanwhile, injuries continued to bother two potential aces: Stan Brown, with a soreness that had kept him on the bench for most of the previous season, and Rob Burgess, with a torn muscle that would keep him sitting next to his buddy Stan until at least April. Chuck Linhardt was hoping to realize fully the potential he had shown in his first two years as a starter, and a kid named Erik Sonberg, a freshman who, two years later, would be picked over Roger Clemens in the MLB draft, was ready to show his stuff. Still, there was Heinkel. There was Hayes.

The mound staffs of the 1978–82 teams were composed of a few deceptive placement pitchers among fireballing wild men—guys who threw until they could throw no more.

At a lanky 185 pounds, Don Heinkel understood the mixing of pitches, and he had combined a hard-breaking curve, a slider, a couple off-speed pitches and some surprising heat for a sterling 14-3 record in the 1980 season on an even shinier 1.74 ERA. Just a game behind at 13-3, rocket man Terry Hayes needed only a bit more predictable control to win his coach's full confidence, his high hard ones sometimes just a little too high. Terry's 2.99 ERA had delivered more than enough defense in the company of booming Shocker bats, with one four-game stretch of more than thirty shutout innings. "Hayes has been inconsistent, but when he's on he's as good as there is," said Coach Stephenson.

While Gene was speaking of Terry Hayes, he might just as well have been referring to outfielder Joe Carter, the two-time All-American and one of the most threatening hitters in collegiate baseball. A hardworking athlete of the first rank only a few months away from a certain introduction to the big time, Joe brought along a .432 average with fifteen round-trippers and ninety-one RBIs from the season previous, an off year for the slugger, whose numbers as a freshman were even higher.

And were it not for lessons learned from their dad, Gene might have tossed a little hyperbole at his brother, Mr. Phil Stephenson of Guthrie, Oklahoma, who in the '80 campaign spent almost as much time as a runner at first base as he did fielding that position. As the team's leadoff hitter, perhaps the most physically imposing leadoff hitter in amateur baseball, Phil put himself on base an astonishing fifty-eight times out of every one hundred at bats. He walked eighty times in 1980, his eye for the strike zone complementing his .410 average when he did decide to swing the bat. Phil pounded fifteen homers, drove in sixty-five runs and led the team in runs scored, with 104 touches at the plate. Meanwhile, his brother was looking for a replacement for Phil in the one-hole, anyone capable of getting on base almost as much as he had, so that Phil's slugging could be even more productive two or three slots down in the lineup. Early speculation suggested that Keith Jones take over in the leadoff slot, the better to use Keith's sprinter speed. "But Keith drew only fifteen walks all of last season," his coach demurred. "He has to learn to be more selective in the pitches he likes," this even as Gene salivated at the thought of Keith Jones taking a big lead off any bag in sight. "He's one of the fastest base runners in collegiate baseball," Keith's thirty-two stolen bases in 1980 proof of his speed, his savvy.

Back to the coach and his worries for a moment. Bob Bomerito, he of the unknown and unknowable nerve injury, would have to play every day at third, no longer able to rest his throwing arm as the Shocks' designated hitter. After missing all of the 1979 season, Bob hit .401, a spectacular number for any player in full possession of his physical powers but an absolutely incredible number for a young man with the dominant side of his body nagged by synapses that refused to fire. Before the injury, Bob Bomerito was stepping into fastballs with the force and the heft of a young Mickey Mantle, parking balls out in territory where only Joe Carter routinely hit. In 1980, Bob hit just four homers and drove in just fifty-five runs—solid numbers, for sure, but far below the slugging that he had shown in his first year at WSU.

Bomerito at third would then join Jimmy Smith (.351 in 1980) at short, Jim Thomas (.347) at second and Phil Stephenson at first. Charlie O'Brien, hitting .331, was slated to start behind the plate. Gene's worries went past third base, however, as he mulled the possible positional switch between Thomas and Smith. Sore-armed Smitty had committed twenty-two errors at shortstop, and his throwing problems argued even more for a twenty-foot move to his left. With Smith stationed at second base, Thomas would move to shortstop. His coach noted, "If Jim Thomas shows he can play well at shortstop, it can do nothing but enhance his chances in the pro draft." Well and good, but with two arms out of three being a bit suspect, Stephenson had to hope that most ground balls off opponents' bats would be hit squarely at the far-ranging Jimmy T.

The outfield, on the other hand, was replete with speed, glued gloves and throwing arms capable of stopping any base runner mid-stride. In a set of choices not theretofore available to Gene, he could on any given day pick and choose among Joe Carter, the bullet Keith Jones, hard-hitting Tim Tolin and Kurt Bradbury and a new arrival out of Nebraska, a superb athlete named Kevin Penner.

In the dying days of a Kansas winter, baseball was about to bloom again in a season full of hope and potential—a season that even an already crusty young coach was forced to admit that this, this right here, might be the Shockers' time.

OFF TO ARIZONA IN SEARCH OF A MIRACLE

A couple logistical notes here, notes that provide a workable overview of the state of baseball at Wichita State University in March 1981. First, the Shocks would board a plane to fly to Arizona for the season-opening road swing, gone now the drafty old vans driven hundreds of miles down into west Texas for away games; second, the day before boarding that plane, the Shocks practiced in a junior high gym—they hit balls into a net strung across the creaky old wood floors of Mathewson Junior High Gymnasium. In three years, Gene Stephenson had brought WSU baseball to a number-six national ranking (*Collegiate Baseball* magazine poll) and had won sufficient respect from university administration for a budget that allowed some air travel—if Gene and his players were able to sell enough raffle tickets to pay for their airfares. But no Shocker, coach or player, had yet to find a long-term workable way around the exigencies of Kansas weather, such climatic nonsense as a single-digit cold snap the week of Opening Day. There was nothing to do but load up the bat bags and take some swings over at Mathewson.

Limbering up down in the desert sun in anticipation of this tough team from Kansas were the nines from Grand Canyon University, Northern Arizona and Arizona State, the Sun Devils ranked twelfth by *Collegiate Baseball*. Grand Canyon had won the NAIA championship in 1980 but had lost seven of its eight .300 hitters to graduation. Poor Northern Arizona,

24-28 the year before, had announced that the university would be dropping baseball after the 1981 season, a reminder to Gene and his troops just too creepy for words.

Gene's take on the first six games of the season: "Winning one game at this time of the year against Arizona State would be a miracle." Jim Thomas, the erstwhile best second baseman in the country, was a bit more sanguine about the schedule, especially forthright in his analysis of his coach's mindset: "Actually, Gene wants a sweep on this trip. Gene has a way of talking to us…he says we're not looking sharp. But we have a lot of players who are game players. I played on the Boulder, Colorado National Baseball Congress team last summer, and this team at WSU is like playing for a college all-star team." Jimmy offered this expertise to Bob Lutz, staff writer for the *Wichita Eagle*, who promptly shared JT's thoughts with about 100,000 interested readers. Anyone scouring the archives of Kansas newspapers will look in vain for any quotations on the game of baseball from anyone remotely named James Thomas after February 12, 1981.

Some thirty hours later, Wichita State University head baseball coach Gene Stephenson had effectively removed the lateral surfaces of his mouth's mucous membrane. A rapidly aging Gene had bitten his tongue, had chewed his mustache, had swallowed his words until at last he might talk to gathered reporters after the game with Grand Canyon, might talk with the modulation appropriate to a Division I head coach helping to shape the characters of the young men in his charge. "We stunk," he said in his first sentence to the press, Gene always leading with the nicest possible statement he might make. "We stunk the place up. Our guys weren't ready to play. They must have been reading their press clippings. I've never seen a team at WSU play so badly, not even in our first season. It was by far the sorriest offensive exhibition I've seen." The Phoenix beat writer did not use "said" as the verb of choice in relaying Gene's quoted thinking. Rather, the reporter went immediately to "he stormed."

Shut out for the first time in 178 games, the Shocks just could not have disappointed themselves and their coach one error more. As their coach was unafraid to point out, "Carter let two balls go through him. He turned some others into base hits. Jones hit a single and just kept running. They put him out by a mile. Thomas [erstwhile public information officer] let a perfect double-play ball go right through his legs. That would have got us out of the inning. But no, Grand Canyon scores three runs after the error."

The Arizona trip did not end well, not well at all, as the Shocks stumbled to an easy ASU win, the twelfth-ranked Sun Devils coasting to an 11–2 victory, their base paths greased by three Shocker errors and no fewer than ten walks served up by Shocker pitchers. Looking back on the season's beginning, Gene was all back and forth. "We're not used to a losing record," he said. "We played three good games out here and three bad ones. Today was one of the bad ones. We had some control problems with our pitchers, but you have to figure that from us this time of year. Arizona State has been practicing outside every day for months, and we haven't." And then he cleared his throat. Maybe he spat, and he spoke then of losing two out of three to the Sun Devils in front of more than four thousand of their fans sitting in splendor. He thought of Shocker fans back home in the makeshift ballpark with its silly lack of indoor plumbing, its ridiculous deficiencies, like the Arizona losses, "a humbling experience." And maybe he spat again.

Meanwhile, he wondered, why couldn't the weatherman send some sunshine and warm breezes into south-central Kansas this particular February?

STREAKERS!

The month of March represented a team's response to its coach's voiced opinions, as the Shockers began to score, oh, thirty-five runs in a game, even as Shocker pitching healed itself from injuries both physical and mental. WSU extended its record to 19-6, with a perfect 4-0 record in the Missouri Valley. Indeed, good play seemed to be everywhere around the diamond as young Shockers stepped forward to give the veterans some rest in the blowout games. The Shocks shoved their winning streak to seventeen with lopsided wins against South Dakota State, 8–2 and 18–0. Shocker hitting was predictably strong and consistent. Shocker speed belied the Jackrabbits' mascot, as WSU stole a dozen bases on the day, with thirty-seven thefts in the past six games, Gene's lessons of aggression settling in now, running on essentially every game situation second nature to his guys.

But perhaps the big story to come out of these easy wins lay in the lineups themselves, as Gene jockeyed players back and forth to take best advantage of the talent waiting up and down the roster. As the University of Colorado Buffaloes discovered, walking into a meat grinder in their five-game series as they lost by a combined score of 91–10. The destruction raised WSU's record to 24-6, as Gene commented to the press on the last day of March, "We're now playing the way we knew we could all year."

A VALIDATION OF SORTS

The arrival of the University of Hawaii Rainbows at Wichita's Mid-Continent Airport on April 11 was reminiscent of Southern Cal's coming to town two years earlier. Runner-up in the College World Series the previous spring and ranked fourth in the nation on its touchdown in west Wichita, Hawaii, by its very appearance, ratified the stature of the toddling Shocker baseball program. By the time of their departure, the Rainbows had demonstrated a couple truths about WSU baseball almost four years into its rebirth—or half-truths maybe, as in "Good hit, no pitch, no field—on the game days that matter most." Well, sometimes maybe. As on unlucky April 13, when WSU blew a 5–1 second-inning lead, the breakdown a result of errors in the field and a succession of walks and wild pitches from the mound. The Shocks scored a dozen runs against America's fourth-best team but allowed the Rainbows to score eighteen in return, a crystallization of the Wichita State University baseball team's worst days since February 1978.

The gloom over the second game's loss smothered the good feelings brought about by WSU's 10–6 victory the day before. The disappointment obscured the fact that Hawaii was thrilled to be leaving Kansas with a split. Hawaii coach Les Murakami said, "I couldn't be happier for Gene. I couldn't

The nationally ranked University of Hawaii came to Wichita in 1980 and was happy to leave town with a split in the two-game series.

be happier for myself. If we had to split, it was perfect. He won the first one in front of a large crowd [on Sunday evening at Lawrence-Dumont]. We won the last game with not so many fans on hand to witness WSU's loss [on Monday afternoon at Shocker Field]." Coach Murakami kindly did not mention the holes at the field's edges, the beginnings of long-promised dugouts. "But why dig the holes now, with a nationally prominent team in town?" That was the question on everyone's mind. Some possible answers spoke of administrative ill will.

With the Rainbows gone, the Shocks proceeded to destroy visiting opponents, using every component of the game—pitching, fielding, throwing, hitting, running—to their best advantage. In one game against Loyola Marymount, Gene's speedsters stole sixteen bases and were thrown out only once.

Amid the team success came record-book personal achievements as well, as on the afternoon of April 29, in the fourth inning of the Shockers' game against Oklahoma City University, with Phil Stephenson at bat, OCU's Randy Tiemann's pitch came—per Phil—"right there" on a three-one count, but Phil "didn't get the bat open to hit it square," and he was left to hope that "the ball would fall in." Fall in it did, just over shortstop, as his bloop single began a two-run rally and simultaneously established an NCAA record of forty-six straight games in which Phil had hit safely. Then, with another single in the second game of the double-header, the streak stretched to forty-seven, a game won easily by the Shocks, 7–1. Typically, Gene talked about subjects other than his brother's heroics. "In the first game [also a victory, 5–3], I was very pleased with our pitching, but we didn't compete offensively. We just didn't hit the ball like we're capable."

In the next game out, versus Oklahoma State at Lawrence-Dumont, Phil Stephenson hit three line drives directly at high-jumping Cowboy infielders and drew one of his perennial walks. His record hitting streak ended at last.

ON BEING TIRED

Shocker pitching, for all its flashes of low-hit brilliance, was getting tired. One score, this against Creighton on May 3, demonstrated the full effect of the collective exhaustion. Blue Jays 23, Wichita State 22. How in the name of all that's rosined and spat upon does a team score twenty-two runs in a

In each of their late season runs, the Shockers struggled to keep pitchers healthy. These were guys who refused to back off on any pitch, any game.

collegiate baseball game and still lose? On the reasonably healthy side, the starters—Don Heinkel, Terry Hayes, Bryan Oelkers and Erik Sonberg—were able to do the job, able to do it very well when their stuff was working, when their curveballs were finding the strike zone, when the off-speed pitches had opposing batters lunging in futility. On those other days, though, the afternoons when the starter found himself unable to coax another inning, another pitch, when a complete game was just not going to happen, Coach Stephenson found himself with two choices: Bruce Morrison or Joe Krisik. Joe unable to straighten his throwing arm, such was the pain shooting from his shoulder, and Bruce, who never whined, saying that he would throw until he couldn't throw again. With the valley tournament looming and the prospect of a return to Omaha hinging almost entirely on the pitching keeping pace with the hitting, the Shocks and their coaches worried that even a .389 team batting average might not be enough.

Even though larger drool buckets were being issued to the pro scouts in town to watch Joe Carter and other Shocker stars.

JOE BTFSPLK

Computer-generated graphics lay far in the future when the *Wichita Eagle* published its clip-art illustration of Coach Stephenson standing, hand to his chin, looking uncertain at best, a cartoonish black cloud spewing rain on his W-hatted head. This was the *Eagle*'s adaptation of Al Capp's lightning-struck and perpetually showered-upon character, Joe Btfsplk. Wet as he may have been from the rain-soaked MVC tournament, Gene was deep in thought, certain that better times lay ahead. "It's almost as if somebody more powerful than us wanted it that way," he philosophized after Southern Illinois bounced back from the Shocks' 23–4 demolition of the Salukis on Friday to take the Missouri Valley Conference title after 5–3 and 3–0 victories over WSU on Sunday. "I think it might have been for the best. Maybe there's a greater meaning behind all this. I think good will come of it. It can make us a little hungrier, a little more determined."

Divine intervention or not, the upsets brought their own sort of astonishment, their own consequences, not all of which—from a Shocker point of view—were untoward. Their coach talked to the press again, suggesting that the team didn't really put that much stock in another MVC tournament crown, having won the tourney the year before. "Frankly, the Missouri Valley championship doesn't mean that much to the players," Gene said. "Anyway, we just didn't play well, and the ball bounced right to them and the ball bounced away from us. They [SIU] didn't hit the ball hard all day, but they hit to all the right spots. Talk about a game of inches…but that's baseball. That's the way it goes."

The way the NCAA tournament selection went, WSU won—big time. The Shockers—now 55-13—were assigned to the Atlantic Regional, where they would meet 34-22 Clemson in the first-round game, with Mississippi State (42-15) and East Tennessee State (40-13) warming up in the wings. The Shockers were not assigned to the Midwest Regional, down in Tulsa, at Oral Roberts University's home field—speaking of higher powers. In its wisdom, the NCAA selection committee sent the losing Shockers back east, while the winning Salukis stayed in the Midwest to begin a rougher road to Omaha. "The Midwest Regional looks mean," Gene said. "SIU is definitely man-for-man the weakest team in it, but that doesn't mean they're not going to win, because they were also the weakest team here [the MVC tournament]." Gene's objective analysis then turned personal: "Besides, I don't like ORU. I don't like the thought of playing there. I don't like the field. We've never played well there."

A Digression upon Relations Between the Baseball Program and the Athletic Department

The clashes with the athletic department came big and small, many of them downright petty. Such was the case on a May day in 1981 when the athletic director's secretary, a territorial sort of secretary who wielded muscle far beyond her job title—"more of a henchman, with a terrible disposition," the general opinion of the baseball program—announced that Wayne Harmon, the team's trainer, would not be making the trip to Clemson, South Carolina, for the Shockers' first games in the regionals of the College World Series. Rather, the athletic department had decided that Doug Vandersee, the basketball trainer, would be going in Wayne's place. "Doug is a fine and accomplished trainer," Gene says, "but he hadn't spent a minute with our players. He didn't know their individual needs, the injuries they were fighting. And I understood that the athletic department was just dinking with us, just showing us again who was in charge, who would eventually make every last decision—even down to who was taping ankles for our players. That woman was just trying to show us once more that baseball didn't matter in the athletic department or in the university at large."

So Gene ordered the team and staff (minus one) all aboard while he made a phone call. He announced to the athletic department that the team bus would not be driving to the airport until Mr. Wayne Harmon, trainer, climbed on. Some tense moments passed as the Shockers' bus sat in the parking lot at Henry Levitt Arena, its diesel engines idling as some nervous administrators across campus hurried Wayne toward a bus ride. The last word from the trumped, sulking secretary? "We hope that the baseball team drops off a cliff in South Carolina and never comes back."

Of Publicity and Pitchers

The Shocks moved into the regional tournament in something of a funk at the plate—funky, at least, for a team batting almost .400, leadoff hitter to ninth man. Having lost two in a row at Shocker Field, something of a hitter's park, most especially with Kansas's predominant south wind blowing, WSU now faced the prospect of solving its slump at Clemson Baseball Field, with its four-hundred-foot fences, and prevailing winds blowing smack into a

Phil Stephenson, boasting a rare combination of strength, speed and a high baseball IQ, was the 1982 College Player of the Year.

batter's face. Consider this: of the Clemson Tigers' fifty-six home runs on the season, only twelve came at home. Joe Carter wasn't bothered. "No, we're not in a slump," he said matter-of-factly. "It's nothing we can't work out. If we're not going to be able to hit a lot of homers, we'll just spray the ball around." Bruce Morrison seconded his buddy: "We're not in a slump, just a little rut."

Slump, rut, ditch, wrinkle—no matter, the sports media in Clemson, South Carolina, was spilling gallons of ink in advance of the Shockers' arrival in town for the first regional game against the Tigers, WSU bats being the subject of almost all the anticipated consternation. Seems the Carolinians couldn't very well imagine some young guns batting .384 as a team, couldn't see how some guy named Stephenson could be hitting safely essentially every other time at bat against some of the best pitching in collegiate baseball, couldn't possibly understand how a football recruit could be showing Major League numbers (119 runs batted in) in what amounted to way less than a Major League number of games. So busy was Clemson sports talk with Shocker batsmanship that the pundits forgot all about Shocker pitching.

The next day, Don Heinkel stomped to the mound and threw a two-hitter at Clemson and at the press who had ignored him and his fellow hurlers from Kansas. "Shockers KO Clemson 7–2" read the headline back home, "Heinkel Stars," the subhead. Don's performance was all the more timely, considering Gene's decision to start him came at a very late moment. Terry Hayes had been the announced starter, but while watching Clemson batting practice, the coach noticed that they were cracking fastballs with particular furor; immediate decision—pitch Heinkel and his breaking stuff. And his changeups accounted for much of the Clemson outage in the latter innings. "I caught my rhythm today," said Heinkel.

Oh yeah, the beer joke.

After the game, Clemson's veteran coach, Bill Wilhelm, mused [the reporter's word, "mused"], "Was that guy's name 'Heineken' or 'Lowenbrau'?"

BAD JOKE, ALL RIGHT

The Shockers' 1981 season ended on May 24, a long baseball day, in a game that stretched for thirteen innings after four hours of hard, back-and-forth baseball. The Shockers played well, fought hard and harder still, as their hitting slump persisted and scoring opportunities disappeared. All the while, freshman right-hander Frank Schulte pitched his heart out, allowing only two runs in his seven innings on the mound. With their legendary power hitting absent, the Shocks clawed for every advantage. "We tried to run. We tried to bunt. We tried everything," Gene said. "Everything just backfired."

His assessment might have extended to the team's last four games, in which the Shockers batted but .200, averaged seven hits and scored sixteen runs all told. Most telling in the East Tennessee game, WSU hitters went down, in order, in six innings. Six! The fearsome WSU attack coming up with blanks in six full innings was a lapse unheard of in the regular season.

First-team all-conference players returning from the 1980 season. *Back row, left to right*: Don Heinkel, Bob Bomerito, Joe Carter and Terry Hayes. *Front row, left to right*: Jim Thomas, Coach Gene Stephenson and Phil Stephenson.

The thoughts of everyone associated with Wichita State baseball, the thoughts of every casual fan, every now-and-then reader of the local sports pages, coalesced in a headline from the *Wichita Eagle* on the morning of June 1, 1981: "WSU Baseball at Crossroads After 4 Years." The opinion piece, written by staffer Bob Lutz, mixed its metaphors heavily in the first sentence, but the implication was nonetheless clear: "The Wichita State baseball program, after four years of smooth sailing, has come to its first fork in the road." A third and a fourth metaphor in the second and third sentences identified the focus of both the program's proven accomplishments and its looming problems. "Coach Gene Stephenson had put Shocker baseball on the map with magnificent recruiting. But it'll take a year of recruiting to beat all years to keep WSU on the winning road, or the Shocker baseball program could start to put on the brakes."

As Writer Lutz put it so bluntly, "What makes Stephenson's accomplishments so overwhelming is that he has recruited such quality players to such a second-class program." And, of course, Mr. Lutz went directly to the facilities, or lack thereof: "The team plays at Shocker Field without any permanent seating, restrooms, dressing rooms, or press box." And he might have added to his description "a second-class program in a cold climate," the recruitment of pitchers made extra unlikely to a ballpark without indoor plumbing in a place whose pipes would have been frozen anyway. "Many top high-school players opt for a warmer climate to play collegiately. Especially pitchers, whose arms can be racked by cool weather." The nub of Gene's recruiting dilemma: to sell his program now—right now—without a stadium and, as Bob Lutz would have it, "without first-class treatment from the WSU athletic department," which rushed forward immediately to defend itself, citing "other priorities" and suggesting that "baseball's needs are no bigger than those of football and basketball." To which any WSU baseball fan might reply, "Obviously" in the matter of priorities and "Ha!" in the matter of relative need. The column went on to spell out the details of the difficulty, most especially in the impending loss of the team's offensive firepower, both to graduation and to the prospect of professional contracts. As Bob Lutz reminded his readers, "The Shocks stand to lose the players who belted 87 of the team's 113 homers during the 1981 season and who drove in 583 of the 755 runs."

What, then, were the alternatives?

Recruit some power hitters in a fat hurry?

Become a defensive team, relying more on pitching and golden gloves than on hitting to win games?

The operative word in this entire discussion? "Recruiting."

PAPER PROMISES

In 1978, the team played its home games at McAdams Park, on east Thirteenth Street, a neighborhood field eventually made famous by Barry Sanders, the National Football League Hall of Famer who practiced his cuts and feints on the gridiron just next door. There was not one thing wrong with McAdams; it was a swell enough high school ballpark, but not a place the Shocks could get emotional about, not a home field. Not by a stretch. Still, the South Diamond at McAdams did offer the players seating much like that of a slow-pitch softball field (benches behind chain-link fencing), a luxury not forthcoming at their eventual on-campus field. The outfield lights were serviceable, the bleachers were sufficient to the first-year baseball crowds and there was a nice, if badly unpredictable grass infield, bad hops waiting to jump in a shortstop's face without warning. But in no way imaginable was McAdams Park the facility to which Gene's rookie class had been recruited. In his letter to prospective players, Gene wrote exactly what he had been promised. He told his recruits what the university had told him. He did not exaggerate, nor did he qualify. Collegiate Division I athletes might legitimately expect facilities commensurate with the level of play, and so Coach Stephenson repeated the guarantees he had been given:

> *By the fall of this year* [1978], *we will have our new diamond ready. It will be surrounded by an eight-foot chain-link fence (with warning track) and will have a "hitter's background" (a 30x50 structure) behind the fence in center field. There will be a framed batting tunnel (enclosed for hitters) complete with bullpen mounds and home plates. We will have at least one pitching machine (possibly two) and all the necessary protective screens.*
>
> *By next spring, we will have permanent seating to accommodate up to 4,000 people, a press box, new restrooms, and a concession stand. All of this will be structured on a beautiful site adjacent to the university golf course on campus.*

Or so he had been told.

Necessarily, Gene recruited from a rendering. Using the architectural drawings for the promised stadium and surrounding facilities, he showed high school ballplayers and their families the stuff of what might be, the promise of a new ballpark hanging right there in midair. As the great Joe Carter said later, he a member of Gene's second recruiting class, "When I first looked at this picture of a new stadium, I didn't realize I was going to have to help pay for it."

After the 1978 football season, Gene, working alone, removed the tarps hanging from the end-zone fences at Cessna Stadium, hauling them by hand over to the baseball field, where he hung them over the chain link, obscuring at least in part the play on the field, six-foot tarps covering an eight-foot fence. The closest public restrooms waited at some gas station up or down Twenty-first Street. But Gene had brought in a flatbed trailer, had hauled over the sideline bleachers used for the football team's practices. In so many ways, the Shockers' field resembled a rundown slow-pitch softball facility in a city with massive budgetary problems.

And so Athletic Director Bredehoft voted to give away the tickets to any home game. "But I insisted that we charge a buck to watch a game," Gene says. "We had to assign some value to what we were doing. Even if people were less than comfortable physically, we were putting first-rate collegiate athletics on the field. You don't give the game away." Gene went to work on the field, mowing such grass as might have been indigenous there, dragging hoses, doing it all, this the area where golfers had formerly practiced their irons before a round at the next-door university course.

The promised new facility, with its big-deal Astroturf infield, was pegged at $380,000 with an originally promised opening date of mid-March, the

Coach Stephenson forwarded the promises made to him, recruiting in part on the field-that-was-to-be. Someday. Maybe.

nearby Friends University Falcons the honored opponent in the first Wichita State University home baseball game in eight years. Bad weather had settled in, the late winter crud hauled in by the forty-mile-per-hour winds that routinely whipped through the city in its breeziest month.

The construction process was given a window of opportunity when the team left town for eleven days, off to play warm-weather schools with completed playing fields and hundreds of fans sitting in real grandstands. The stadium was again promised to be ready on the Shocks' return, but the three vans carrying some exhausted ballplayers arrived in a parking lot opening on a baseball field still weeks away from being in any way playable. No warning track. No fences on the far side of the track. No fences at all. No Astroturf on the infield. And, as would be the case for a very long time to come, no dugouts, no bleachers and nothing approaching a place in which the players could dress.

And so the team had played through the early weeks of the 1978 season, enjoying such success as might be expected of a first-year program, playing to a 7-9-1 record without a true home game yet enjoyed, situational irony everywhere a roaming center fielder might look. In one of the principal contradictions of the 1978 Shocker season stood the scoreboard. The first component of the promised new stadium to be completed, the scoreboard flaunted its black-and-gold chutzpah along Twenty-first Street with its face seemingly reaching one thousand feet into the Kansas sky. Imposing enough up close, Shocker fans still complained, "Yeah, but you can't see it from McAdams Park."

NO PLACE LIKE HOME

Fast-forward a full year, and nothing has changed except that artificial turf now lay on the infield. In a pre-season column, the *Wichita Eagle* reported, "There is no apparent progress in building a stadium to go along with the Shocker baseball field on 21st Street." The university administration had pleaded sudden impoverishment as the rationale for the athletic department's inability to keep a promise, an odd claim indeed for a department that found plenty of money to fire a legendary basketball coach (Harry Miller) and then pay major bucks to his replacement (Gene Smithson); no shortage of scratch to fire the coach (Jim Wright) in a struggling football program, buy out his contract and then throw Oklahoma sorts of dollars at new coach

Willie Jeffries; and certainly no worry about funding for the replacement of the admittedly ragged and faded artificial turf in Cessna Stadium with a superb new all-natural surface.

That newspaper column bemoaned the possibility that "Wichita State could ruin the admirable momentum it has built up with the new baseball program if some kind of permanent structure isn't started soon." And columnist Randy Brown was just warming up: "Besides, the field looks silly the way it is now. There's that nifty playing surface, that awesome scoreboard, and no place to sit. Or write a story. Or set up a broadcast booth. Or buy soda pop. Or go to the bathroom. It's hard to imagine Ted Bredehoft passing up this kind of chance to sell stuff."

Mr. Bredehoft at last stepped forward to say that Wichita State's new baseball stadium still stood one more long year away, the spring of 1980 assuredly a grand time for the first home game there, a mere $1.2 million necessary to be found in the meantime. "Pressed for a timetable of activities leading to the construction, he admits that it's indefinite," the newspaper said. "Originally, I had planned to use baseball to develop a third revenue sport," he said but claimed that fundraising had been slowed, the money funneled off to the revamp of Cessna Stadium. "We cannot produce any revenue from baseball without a stadium and lights," the illumination alone projected to require $170,000 from the university's coffers.

Gone now was the athletic director's original plan to build the stadium a section at a time, even if the first section might include locker rooms for the players. For whatever reasons, Mr. Bredehoft simply pronounced section-by-section construction "not practical right now."

The 1979 Missouri Valley Conference baseball tournament had been scheduled to run May 18–21 in Wichita to showcase the new stadium. Instead, the tourney moved to good old Lawrence-Dumont in downtown Wichita. The absence of a stadium was costing the university and the community in other ways, as even Ted Bredehoft had to admit: Wichita State had enjoyed a solid chance to land the NCAA Midwest Regional, pending the completion of a stadium. Gene admits to some naïveté in this regard. "I had always operated on the assumption that when a man makes you a promise, he's going to do everything in his power to keep that promise," he said. "Especially in an institutional setting, with the full weight of the university seemingly standing behind the promise, I saw no reason to doubt."

In November 1980, the forty members of Gene's first "Home Run Club" had each given $1,000 to build dugouts; a group of generous, farsighted people gave their money to the designated use of the baseball team. By April

HOME RUN CLUB

In 1980 a group of individuals interested in furthering the successes of the Wichita State baseball program was formed and became known as the Home Run Club. Because of their effort and contributions, a home and visitor dugout was constructed. These dugouts, still in their original location, were the cornerstones on which Eck Stadium and Tyler Field were built. The following names are the original members of the Home Run Club:

Todd Aikins	Bill Eckert	Nelson Hobart
Buck Alley	Byron Eschelman	Dr. Eugene Kaufman
George Angle	George Fahnestock	B. J. Kingdon
Harold Bauer	Dr. George Farha	Dr. Sam Kouri
Dr. Roger Bond	Larry Fleming	Bob Sayre
Dewey Brittain	Daniel E. Foley	Terry Scanlon
Earl F. Callison, Jr.	Robert A. Geist	Maxine Scott
Doug Clarke	Theodore Gore	Howard Sherwood
Bill Cohen	Jim Grady	Quincy Utter
Al Conner	L. C. Harmon	Bud Vann
Dr. Ray Cook	Willis E. Hartman	Jerry Williamson
William V. Darling	Charles E. Henning	Herb Wishengrad

In October 1980, Coach Stephenson found forty faithful supporters of the team to donate $1,000 each for the construction of dugouts. The $40,000 quickly disappeared into the bowels of the administration, and six months later, there were still no dugouts.

1981, nothing had happened, and there was no sign of construction about to begin. Buck Alley was president of the club, and he saw the proceeds of their giving essentially seized by the university, President Clark Ahlberg way out front. "He nixed our fundraising," Alley said. "We were all so disappointed. Just lock, stock and barrel. Gene is a super person, and the city is going to lose this program if something isn't done."

As it became obvious that the money had gone elsewhere, Gene could remain silent no longer. The immediate impetus for going public arrived with the University of Hawaii baseball team. The runner-up in the 1980 College World Series, the Rainbows arrived for a two-game series. The first game was played at Lawrence-Dumont Stadium, the grand old ballpark on the west bank of the Arkansas River as it flows through Downtown Wichita, the second game to follow on campus. When Gene came out to the university field the following morning, he discovered that a stray backhoe had dug holes for the beginnings of dugout construction. With America's second-best collegiate team in town, the university had decided to make a statement. What else, Gene wondered, other than spite could explain the piles of dirt, the absurd ditches just outside the first- and third-base lines? "The university was effectively telling us that a baseball field was not wanted in this particular place, that the president had put a stop on every last thing we were trying to do out here."

The cars immediately behind the Shocker dugout belonged to the players, and necessarily so. They changed into their uniforms in their vehicles.

Right away, Gene took the discussion out toward words whose consequences typically involve such descriptions as "gross insubordination," "inappropriate publicity" and "immediate dismissal." But not before he set benches in front of the excavations and—what else—played ball. As the head baseball coach took his case to the fans, as he began to speak openly about broken promises, frustration set in on another front. It seems that the university had undertaken a $300,000 fundraising campaign in support of a new physical education facility on campus, a move that would have made asking for money from supporters doubly difficult in the case of a new baseball stadium, at least in the mind of Ted Bredehoft, who began to stutter and stumble about in a discussion of overpopulated stoves. "Certain things have to be put on the back burner sometimes," he said. "If you get other things on the front burner waiting, well, in my opinion, all of our activities are on the front burner. It just gets a little crowded." And then, in one of the more debatable of his pronouncements, Ted Bredehoft said, "I want a new stadium—more than the head coach."

Even the most zealous of the athletic director's supporters might have balked at Mr. Bredehoft's suggestion that his desire for bathrooms exceeded Gene's. The players, meanwhile, had reached new depths of cynicism—even with new dugouts under alleged construction, the forms for pouring concrete rising out of the ground in an ill-conceived bit of mid-season timing with NCAA Division I games being played by a national powerhouse a few feet away. Crude, durable and little else, the dugouts—according to rumors the players themselves were hearing—would include no water fountain, would hold no bat racks, would not even have a locker for hanging their warm-up jackets. "I hear the dugouts will be just shells," one anonymous player told a reporter. Another unnamed player chimed in, "And what a time to build them, here in the middle of the season." In fact, E.W. Johnson Construction, a regular WSU contractor, was merely converting a couple concrete box-culverts into dugouts.

Big-hitting Bruce Morrison, who came all the way from Long Island to play for the Shockers, didn't mind speaking on the record. "It was really an inviting thing when they told us what this stadium would be," the designated hitter said. "Then when I came here, it was a rude awakening. We didn't have a field. About half the time we were practicing on the girls' field or any piece of land we could find. I remember I met Ted in his office, and he just laid it on me. He told me he came from Arizona State and that he wanted to have a baseball program like they had there. Now it's four years later, and they've just started building dugouts!"

The flashy scoreboard immediately became a structural anomaly, standing above outfield weeds, chain-link fences and no dugouts whatsoever.

By the middle of the 1981 season, the frustration was palpable, players openly expressing their dismay over the failure of a stadium to appear. "Shocker Field Is Just That—A Field and Nothing Else" read the headline in the *Wichita Eagle* for Monday, April 27. Staff writer Bob Lutz's subhead was even more pointed: "False Promises Have WSU Baseball Players Feeling like Suckers." Pitcher Rob Burgess, injured at the time of the article, was quoted in his disbelief, "There's a $200,000 scoreboard [Rob exaggerated by one hundred large here], a $100,000 artificial turf infield. And there are one-dollar seats."

The scoreboard did indeed stand out as a particular anomaly, its sheer mass an insult of sorts to the squirming. The athletic department had brought in a bulkheaded railroad car (#SFTZ301050), its paint badly chipped and its Santa Fe logo scarred and peeling, on which the butt-freezing and leg-numbing might begin. There had been no corporate offers to underwrite a grandstand for Shocker Field, no rush of individual contributions to put some high-dollar seats in the house. Understandably, the soft-drink company that paid for the scoreboard was interested in selling soda pop, an endeavor not particularly supported by three or four rows of two-by-twelves on a metal stair-step frame. And so the state-of-the-science electronics flashing and informing outside the left-field fence stood there, the largest scoreboard in collegiate baseball, a laughing, jeering slap in the face to the players and fans promised a four-thousand-seat stadium with all attendant luxuries.

Original Shocker Chuck Linhardt took the lapse personally. "Bredehoft had a lot of us into his office that first year and told us what he going to do with the stadium," he told the newspaper. "I understand there have been problems. But they shouldn't be promising stuff and not coming through." Chuck did not pull his punches. "I was a sucker to become a Shocker." "A lot of us change our clothes in our cars in the parking lot before a game," chimed in center fielder Keith Jones. "We're one of the best teams in the nation, and we're still playing sandlot ball." It was tough to argue with old Keith: the Shockers' record stood at 44-9 on that April day in 1981, the team ranked tenth in the country.

The facilities for center fielder Jones's sandlot team included the aforementioned scoreboard and its accompanying irony; the bright-green infield, with its mocking of everything the outfield grass was not; two sets of bleachers on the Santa Fe flatcar, the tiny trailer serving as a press box that effectively blocked all of right field from any vantage point inside; the

The little ticket booth (top left) became home to the PA announcer, the poor person who could not see right field from his seat there. In the foreground is a good example of the bad outfield "grass."

backstop, a chain-link outfield fence; and a PA booth directly behind home plate, a booth that might easily be mistaken for a single-seater outhouse. With no restrooms on site, players and fans alike were forced to use the portable toilets brought in on game days, the Johnnies-on-the-spot serving as a workable metaphor for Shocker home games in the fourth year of Gene Stephenson's promise-keeping.

The fact was that the stadium fell into a financial hole in the years of its promised building, Gene's first year on campus, a now-distant 1978. Bredehoft was quoted in the *Eagle* as saying, "That stadium, in my opinion, would already have been built had it not been for the drought we went through here. As in any business, we went through a few financial dips. The same year we were going to build a stadium, we had a capital-outlay plan on a new track, and we hired new football and basketball coaches. I don't care if you're Notre Dame or USC, when you go through all three of those things during an eighteen-month period, you're going to have a temporary setback." In WSU's case, the "temporary setback" amounted to a $480,000 setback at the end of the 1980 fiscal year. "That forced us to delay any kind of fundraising effort for a baseball stadium," Bredehoft concluded.

In a piece written two years later, the *Wichita Eagle* came forward with a long article on what was perceived to be the resurrection of the sports budget at Wichita State, the newspaper's metaphor the most notorious of flops, the most dangerous of failures. "Raise the *Titanic*," roared the article's first sentence. "Ted Bredehoft sank it a few years ago, when the flamboyant Wichita State University athletic director steered into a fiscal iceberg that ripped a gash in a $300,000 reserve fund and sank his program deep in debt. But the same showboat captain has pried the *Titanic* from the muck at the bottom of the sea, and it's heading for the surface again." Well, maybe, what with the basketball team barred from post-season play and its concomitant revenue—$80,000 in pre-probation 1979—oddly, from Mr. Bredehoft's vantage, not that hurtful.

Chapter 7

PROMISE MADE, PROMISE KEPT

Promised field or no, there was baseball to be played at Wichita State University in the spring of 1982, but five of the top nine hitters on the 1981 team had gone to the pros. And so, naturally, Gene's discussion of the impending season turned, unnaturally, to pitching and defense, which had been solid in the past but would need to be stellar in the next four months. "I think we'll be much deeper in our pitching staff, and hopefully by later in the spring we'll be better in the field," said Stephenson. "I believe we can counteract some of what we've lost." Few teams could lose the firepower now absent from the '82 Shockers and still send such fine line-drive hitters to the plate as Jimmy Thomas (.379, five homers, seventy RBIs), Jim Spring (.367, seven homers, forty-eight RBIs) and consensus All-American Phil Stephenson (.447, sixteen home runs, ninety-two RBIs—while also establishing new NCAA records for runs scored (a crazy 112) and hitting safely in consecutive games (forty-seven). These three returning stars would anchor the infield with junior college transfer Russ Morman rotating with Phil at first base and right field. Sophomore Pat Blasi stood ready to play second, third or short if an off-season shoulder surgery would allow him back. Dave Lucas, another junior college transfer, looked ready to start at shortstop, backed up there by freshman Mark Grogan. Lucas had played summer ball with teammates Stephenson, Thomas and Heinkel for the Fairbanks Alaska Goldpanners, building some chemistry in the process.

With all their outfielders gone to the minor leagues and big-time reserve Tim Tolin now a Shocker graduate assistant, the holes in the grass seemed major. Knowing eyes turned to Kevin Penner, the sophomore all-around athlete who played in fifty-three games in 1981, most of that time at third base, taking his glove and his gun now to left field. Tim Gaskell had played in just nineteen games the year previous, but he batted an even .400 to go with strong fielding and a good arm. Newcomers Loren Hibbs, late of the baseball program at the University of Kansas, and Dennis Overacker, recently of Wichita North High School, were also expected to see frequent action.

The 1982 pitching staff began with the steady, the old reliable, the quietly outstanding Don Heinkel, he of the thirty-five WSU career victories, recently named MVP in the prestigious National Baseball Congress tournament. With the right-handed Heinkel throwing strikes, a pitcher in the most technical and practiced sense of the word as his anchor, Coach Stephenson looked off toward the bullpen and pronounced the 1982 staff "the best we've ever had at Wichita State." Gene smiled at the ERAs of Frank Schulte, Stan Brown and Erik Sonberg, the highest among those three starters a stingy 2.78, a 16-3 record theirs, too. And waiting to emerge into a top Major League draftee stood left-hander Bryan Oelkers, his pitching to build all season long, peaking just when it needed to—in Omaha. Six newcomers, five freshman and a sophomore would compete for roles in relief, bringing newfound depth to a staff nagged in the past two seasons by lingering injuries. Gene saw strong arms in pre-season drills, freshman Jim Daniel weighing maybe 150 pounds but clocking his fastball right at ninety miles an hour. The coach hoped that his youngsters might mature, that they might give Don, Frank, Stan and Erik some rest, some reprieve game to game.

Behind the plate, Charlie O'Brien might hope for little or no respite from long hours on his haunches, Charlie having emerged as a catcher of the first collegiate rank, knowledgeable, self-assured, able to manage pitchers with a hard-won maturity, his bat helping the Shockers in the clutch, ready to perpetuate the offensive threat from the middle of the lineup. Walt Hagerty, who had spelled Charlie so ably in 1981, had injured a knee in summer ball, and Gene had redshirted him, leaving only two untested freshmen behind the overworked O'Brien.

BACK TO YEAR ONE

The talent was raw and untested really, forced all winter to practice in a junior high gym, its sixty-five-foot length barely long enough for the pitchers to throw effectively, the rest of the guys playing catch, a little pepper, a poor approximation of a game meant to be played in sunshine, the Shockers' light and warmth postponed till opening day. In what Coach Stephenson called "better than nothing," the team did drive out north of town for a few afternoons of practice in the pavilions of the Kansas Coliseum, the area's largest concert and exhibition space. The pavilions adjoining the arena on the coliseum complex had been built to host livestock shows, and the Wichita Wings, professional indoor soccer players, had laid some cheap artificial turf on the concrete floors to approximate their arena-sized pitch. And so here was the state of the program—in terms of facilities—in the late winter of 1982: the team enjoyed a nice improvement in their ability to simulate game conditions by moving to an improvised soccer field in a cow barn.

Bring on the big boys!

First up was Arizona State, the WSU athletic director's old school, ranked second in the nation at the time behind Cal State–Fullerton, the Sun Devils easy victors over little Laverne College, a real-time tune-up for a team with a year-round tan, seventeen games already under their uniform belts. Gene talked of potential embarrassment, his ranks depleted, his team unpracticed. There followed in quick succession a same-day game against Grand Canyon University, the NAIA powerhouse, and then two more games in two days against A-State. The Shockers looked exactly like what they were: talented, raw and, now, severely tested.

Arizona State 7, Shocks 1.

Shocks 15, Grand Canyon 2.

Arizona State 3, Shocks 2.

Arizona State 18, Shocks 0.

There was pure, crimson-faced embarrassment in that last score, all right—just three runs scored in total against an admittedly great team. When the score had gone to 17–0, an ASU runner stole second in the bottom of the eighth. WSU went just nuts, livid at the disrespect of these Arizonans, who were playing contrary to the unspoken rules of the game. When the team came into the dugout, preparing to bat in the top of the ninth, Gene gathered the guys around and said, "Men, take that steal as a compliment. Arizona State must recognize that we're perfectly capable of scoring nineteen this inning."

The debacle in the last game against the Sun Devils represented the worst loss suffered in the Stephenson administration, with nine runs scored in a third inning reminiscent of the Shockers in the Carter era, old Indian star Lou Boudreau's son on the mound for the Devils. "Last year, our team would have stayed in a contest like that," Gene said, his big sticks able to come back against essentially any lead.

Up next were the undefeated Texas Longhorns, with big-name pitchers and Major-Leaguers-in-waiting Calvin Schiraldi and Roger Clemens. The two combined for eighteen innings of scoreless baseball against the Shockers down in Austin. It was close enough in the opener, 2–0, with WSU able to muster but one hit against Schiraldi in the collegiate version of a big-time hurler who would play eight years in the Majors. That one hit came from shortstop Dave Lucas, batting ninth in the order, who would go on to have three of the Shockers' six hits in the double-header. In the second game, Clemens needed just one of the twelve runs his teammates gave in support of a right arm that would soon enough earn seven Cy Young Awards.

The Shockers were now 4-6 on the season with an anorexic team batting average of .226, but they were headed home to face the waiting Tigers of Fort Hays State.

THE 1982 WICHITA STATE BASEBALL TEAM, VERSION 2.0

The Tigers didn't know what to think of Erik Sonberg and the aspirin he threw at them that early spring day in Wichita. Brilliant in a three-hit, nine-strikeout, one-walk stunner, Erik would have won going away with but one Shocker run crossing the plate. But no. Shocker bats did a turnaround deal and came out on fire in the team's home opener. Shocker hitters slapped across fifteen runs in the opener to go with Sonberg's complete-game shutout stuff.

The second half of the double-header? More of the same, 12–2, as the Shocks accumulated twenty-seven runs on the day. They used their twenty-six hits to full advantage, taking the extra base, making the most of FHSU errors, pushing the advantage and taking the game to the opposition in the most offensive way possible. It was Geneball all the way. And who should be leading the team at the plate but nine-hole shortstop Dave Lucas, who again went five for seven, continuing the hitting streak that had begun down in Texas. Meanwhile, the entire team looked at the single Sonberg walk and wondered what they might have in Erik, a pitcher for the record books this kid when he was throwing strikes. Day two of the western Kansas university's tour of the big city did not go especially well either, as WSU humiliated the

Tigers 16–0 and 11–1 to sweep the four-game series by the lopsided Little League score of 54–3.

After winning six straight games at home over a long weekend, the Shockers went back on the road for a fourteen-game exodus in which the true character of the '82 team would emerge. The season called for WSU to play New Mexico State and Creighton four times each, these three teams composing the Western Division of the Missouri Valley Conference, and Las Cruces became the hub around which the road trip rotated. Perhaps the offensive production begun at Shocker Field could continue in other teams' ballparks, the seventy-five runs scored in six games an indication of the firepower lurking there. Still, after a sixty-point surge in team batting average, the number stood at just .288, fifty points or so below the heady heights of a year ago. Phil Stephenson was playing essentially perfect baseball, batting .420 and leading the club in hits, home runs, RBIs, total bases, slugging and stolen bases. In one hundred fielding chances at first base and in right field, he had yet to make an error.

Coach Stephenson wasn't sure which of his teams might take the field in New Mexico. Not sure at all. In the first game against the Aggies of NMS, Don Heinkel again pitched brilliantly, a two-hitter this time out, albeit both solo homers, Don throwing but ninety pitches as he ran to sixteen innings his streak of no walks. Shocks 9, Aggies 2.

The next day, March 13, University of Texas–El Paso ace Brian Paper threw a bunch of perfect pitches at Shocker hitters, who whiffed and grounded and popped to the first no-hitter ever thrown against a Wichita State University nine. Enough said. In the second game, the Shockers scored four runs in second-inning revenge and won 7–4.

Red-faced in their hitlessness, sullen in the wither of their coach's disappointment, the Shockers thought and then thought some more about what had been done to them…no, what they had just done to themselves, this inability to reach first base in nine full innings of baseball. These were not pretty thoughts, and the Wyoming Cowboys would be the first victims of this Shocker mindset, upholstered 16–1 by suddenly motivated Shocker batters who, the following day, stuck around Las Cruces to beat the 'Boys again, 5–3.

The Shocker long ball battered Colorado State twice, booming homers from Russ Morman and Phil Stephenson, as did five hard hits from Charlie O'Brien and two triples from Russ. The Shockers won 5–3 and 11–3.

In easily the best performance of the season in the box, WSU exploded for a 24–0 annihilation of the University of Denver, the sixth straight Shocker win. As Bryan Oelkers threw just ninety-three pitches in a three-hitter, every Shocker who was physically able spent time on the diamond.

Stan Brown was throwing hard as well, winner of his fourth straight in the Shocks' 12–3 victory over New Mexico State on the March 19, the Shocks walking away from the competition in fifteen of the last sixteen games. In the next three days, the Shockers would annihilate these reasonably good teams again by a combined score of 36–4. The high-desert sun had felt good on Shocker skin. The chill of Mathewson Gym now forgotten, there was nothing but blue sky and fat pitches. And so when the Shockers returned from their road swing through the Southwest, they found incredulous fans waiting for them. Told that the Shockers would be a defensive team, the folks in the tiny stands had been reading reports of multi-run poundfests, balls hurtling over and into walls, line drives screaming past everyone as the Shockers scored eleven or more runs in butcheries of Wyoming, Denver, Colorado State and New Mexico State, the victims in round-robin play from which they simply could not escape. While not Texas or Arizona State—or Miami or Cal State–Fullerton—on paper, these teams still should have given a rebuilding Shocker program much more difficult opposition. "I don't think people should be deceived into thinking this is a powerful offensive team," Gene said, accused in the newspaper of "looking for a dark cloud inside the silver lining." Maybe so. Maybe it was indeed true that "we scored a lot of runs on that trip, but that's because the pitching staffs we were facing were not very deep." It was also undeniably true that "we've begun to put it together on offense, not with power, but with execution—hitting and running, stealing bases, moving runners along, putting pressure on the opposing team."

And then Gene made another of his occasional prophecies: "What we have here is a team that can be better at playoff time and win more close games."

SORRY, ONLY TWO CLOSE GAMES FORTHCOMING

The critics of Wichita State University's baseball schedule in those early years of the Stephenson era take an academic glee in the games of March 24 to April 5, 1982, happy days for the hometown in which the only schools willing or able to come to cool, cloudy Kansas—even on a home-home deal—were the NCAA Division II-As, the small liberal arts schools nearby, the traveling northern school looking to escape post-winter blizzards. So.

With two exceptions, the final scores will be sufficient to the story, its telling of Shocker athletes coming at just the right moment into their prime.

Baker, Kansas's most expensive private college, dead broke at 29–0 in a nowhere double-header.

Minnesota-Morris, losers of three, 43–15.

Bemidji State, two down, 47–8.

Northeast Oklahoma, ditto, 37–8.

Winona State, alas, 38–4.

Marymount, luckless little Marymount, 22–0 in two games of five innings each.

Back to the exceptions now: William Jewell and Northwest Missouri. On the afternoon of March 28, the Cardinals of WJ from Liberty, Missouri, employed the designated-hitter rule to their fullest advantage, using clutch pitching and a couple timely hits from the cleanup slot to take down the Shockers 5–3. Sure, WSU, deeply offended, came back to pound the Cards 20–1 in the second half of the double-header, but the point was made again: in baseball, on any given day, anyone can beat anyone. Within reason, of course.

Then, on Sunday, April 4, the more than reasonable Bearcats of Northwest Missouri gave the Shockers all they could handle in a two-game split, 4–7 and 8–6. Even in the twilight win, the Shocks had to beat back bases-loaded rallies, as the small school from Maryville refused to go peacefully into that Wichita good night. The Bearcats were kind enough, however, to allow Phil Stephenson a stolen base to bring his season's total to 42, giving him 161 career steals, now just three short of the NCAA record.

Back to league play. The Shockers, winners of four out of four against the NMS Aggies by a combined score of 59–3, set out on another win spree, this one going twenty games before a 3–5 loss to Creighton in the second half of a double-header on April 25, those victories coming in multi-game series against Emporia State, Phillips, Oklahoma City University and the aforementioned Blue Jays from Omaha. Extended hitting streaks were underway as well, from Phil Stephenson and Jim Spring in particular.

Cowboys Up, Sun Devils Down

On April 27, the Cowboys of Oklahoma State came to town, their baseball pedigree a notch or two above the schools' theretofore making their way to Shocker Field. The Pokes had finished second in the 1981 College World

Series, were leading the Big Eight, had won sixteen straight themselves and had beaten WSU soundly in the past three contests between the two teams. With OSU in town, any talk of a Shocker winning streak was way out of line, and the Shocks' rudeness to visiting teams might be coming to end. Or so went the discussion.

Evidently, Erik Sonberg wasn't listening.

The sophomore left-hander from Tulsa gave up two measly little singles over eight innings, while striking out six Cowboy batters. Erik tired in the ninth and gave up three quick runs before being relieved. The WSU lineup had given him eight runs in support, however, and the game was not once close, the Shocks again relying on line drives (ten singles) and team speed (nine stolen bases) to beat "a better team than last year's CWS runner-up," per Gene. "We were very aggressive. I don't think OSU has seen that sort of speed in a while." And suddenly the Shocks looked around at their 55-10 record and saw both the Missouri Valley and NCAA tournaments in the month just ahead.

The interim schedule involved Kansas Newman, Texas Wesleyan, Oral Roberts and Emporia State, only the last-mentioned Hornets giving the Shockers much of a game, taking WSU all the way to a 9–8 come-from-behind squeaker on May 7.

The following day, the Sun Devils of Arizona State, the top-ranked collegiate team in the country, waited for a three-game series, the first game at Lawrence-Dumont Stadium to be televised by ESPN. And so ASU's Chris Johnston stepped to the plate and drove in five runs with his two homers to power Arizona State to a close 9–8 victory. The Shockers were ranked seventeenth going into the game, which was close through the seventh, when Johnston lofted a curveball from freshman reliever Greg LaFever over the left-field fence to score three. The score was back and forth in a game that saw infield hits, wild pitches, diving catches, dropped fly balls, throws straight and hard as a prison term and obvious foul flies blown back forty feet onto the field of play by a Kansas wind laughing at anything like the straight flight of a baseball. Phil Stephenson powered two homers in the game and stole his seventy-ninth base of the season.

And then it was Sunday.

Sunday, May 9, 1982, the day on which the Wichita State University Baseball Shockers announced to the world that they were a team to be recognized in the forthcoming collegiate series of the same name. The headline accompanying the announcement: "Shocks Club Sun Devils in Double-Header Sweep." And indeed they did, the real clubbing coming

For reasons of their own, the players did not like playing at downtown's Lawrence-Dumont Stadium, and they remained essentially homeless for five years.

with timely hits and more base runners on, more Shockers given the go sign, 6 stolen team bases added to the ongoing NCAA record of 291, Arizona States' nine forced errors attributable to the Shocks' willingness to run and run some more. "I could tell by the way they handled themselves that they were afraid of our running game," Gene said afterward. ASU coach Jim Brock concurred, "We couldn't stop them from stealing any base they wanted anytime they wanted."

Line drives and team speed won the two games. Unlike Saturday's loss, in which home run after home run blew out of L-D Stadium, Sunday's victories at Shocker Field arose directly from Gene's philosophies of buck-naked aggression. A grand-slam home run in the final inning of the first game spoiled Don Heinkel's shutout, but he took the victory nonetheless at 15–4. The Shockers hit the ball hard and then ran harder still, twenty-six hits all told, Charlie O'Brien's two-run shot to seal the second game the only WSU homer of the afternoon. So it went, 6–2, the Shockers missing a three-game sweep of the top-ranked Arizona State juggernaut by just a couple runs.

No More Heartache

The 1982 Missouri Valley Conference Baseball Tournament opened in Terre Haute, Indiana, on Friday, May 14, with the top-seeded Shockers bringing a perfect 8-0 record in the Western Division and a third consecutive regular-season championship. WSU would face once more their tourney nemesis, the Salukis of Southern Illinois, who had ripped the Shocks' hearts out but twelve months previous, beating them in two straight games, 5–3 and 3–0. No matter.

The Shockers had Russ Morman this time around, and as the headlines reported, "Morman Saves WSU." And he did, Russ's three-run blast over that Indiana center-field fence giving the Shocks a 9–6 walk-off victory against a team that, in the nine innings previous, had bedeviled them once more, forcing the nation's fourth-ranked team to come back from 4–1 and 6–4 deficits to send the game into the tenth.

Indiana State, the home team, up next, posed no problem whatsoever for Bryan Oelkers, his shutout spoiled in the ninth only by a lucky triple and a sacrifice fly. The Shocks won 13–1 on the strength of Bryan's arm, eleven timely hits, five Sycamore errors and speed. Pure baserunning speed.

The following day, WSU's Charlie O'Brien saw some pitches he liked a lot, as he continued his three-year, one-man battery of Southern Illinois pitching, the Salukis having played their way back through the losers' bracket to again face the Shocks in the tourney's championship game. Catcher O'Brien pounded SIU pitching for a pair of homers, one a grand slam, a sacrifice fly and a well-timed single for an unheard-of eight runs batted in. Batting fifth in the order, Charlie combined with Phil Stephenson in the three-hole and Russ Morman at cleanup to create a collegiate Murderers' Row, as each drove in more than one hundred runs on the season, a feat never before achieved by an NCAA team. Charlie had turned down a contract with the Seattle Mariners a year earlier to return to the Shocker lineup, "and I'm glad I did," he said. "I promised Coach twenty homers and a bunch of RBIs if he'd play me every day."

At tourney's end, the Shockers placed six players on the all-conference first team, Gene was named Coach of the Year in the valley and Phil Stephenson was recognized as the MVC's Player of the Year.

THE BIG TIME, ONE MORE TIME

Wichita Eagle executive sportswriter Randy Brown sat down to his IBM Selectric and pounded out a strong first sentence in a June 7 column on the relative strength of the schedule Gene had put together for the Shockers. "It is time for critics of Coach Gene Stephenson's baseball schedule to stifle themselves," wrote Brown, pointing to the derision of "many who have said that the Shockers grew fat on the Northeast Oklahomas and Winona States of the world." Conceding that WSU's early departures from post-season play in the '80 and '81 seasons did not clarify the argument much, he did remind his readers that three of every four teams in the NCAA playoffs necessarily, mathematically, faced a similar fate. "Now," he wrote, "the Shockers have proven beyond doubt that they are not softies when it comes to scheduling or whipping up on the big boys of the college game."

In a preview of the College World Series, when third-ranked California State University–Fullerton came to town, the Shockers—then ranked but a notch lower nationally—set out to show the homefolks a thing or two in a three-game series, each game being decided in the ninth inning. "Didn't he play today?" was his coach's rhetorical question in reference to third baseman Jim Spring and his performance in the second game of the series. "It was just fitting that he got an opportunity to win the game for us today," as indeed Jim did, with a two-out, bases-loaded single in the ninth inning, the second time in as many days that the Shocks relied on the last at-bat to win. Over at the hot corner, Jim's vacuum of a glove sucked up every ball in the zip code. Soft-spoken, quiet, intent on the job at hand, Jim Spring "showed up every day and practiced hard," per his infield partner Jim Thomas. "This club is something else," Gene spoke of his guys. "We were dead and buried."

Then came the ninth inning, with CSF leading 2–0.

Dave Lucas hit an opposite-field single with one out, bringing up leadoff hitter Jimmy Thomas, who ran the count full before taking a fastball down and in off toward McLean Boulevard past the right-field fence at Lawrence-Dumont. Ballgame tied. Next up was Loren Hibbs, who hit a single up the middle. Phil Stephenson then ripped a double in the left-center gap, but Hibbs was thrown out at the plate on the relay. (Luckless Loren had also been picked off third base after his first-inning triple.) Then, in one of those instances of being too baseball-smart by half, over-thinking Cal State intentionally walked both Russ Morman and Charlie O'Brien in order to pitch to Jim Spring, who, at a fine .312, brought along the lowest average among the Shocker regulars.

Strategy, schmategy.

Jim slapped the first pitch he saw past a diving Fullerton first baseman, and Phil Stephenson waltzed home with the winning run. "Gene told me to go for it if the pitch was there," Jim said afterward, the hit saving Bryan Oelkers, whose five-hit performance deserved a win for sure. The Shocks had won three out of three against the team that, in about ten days, they would see again.

Would see up in Omaha.

THE BEST PITCHING IN THE COUNTRY

The Shocks waited around for a week to learn who might be their first opponent down in New Orleans, the neutral site chosen for the NCAA's fourth-ranked baseball team. Per the policy established in the organization's basketball tournament, the best teams would play their regional contests in a location less rabid than anyplace close to home.

And so at last it was on to the Big Easy to take on Jackson State. "I feel really confident about this team," Gene said, his confidence building as he watched three golden arms loosen up in the heat and humidity of N'awlins. "If our pitchers are healthy, there isn't a college tournament in the world that we can't win." Heinkel, Oelkers and Sonberg would be the starters.

First up was Don Heinkel, who set the champions of the Southwestern Athletic Conference down in a three-hit performance that saw only one of those hits go beyond the infield as the Shocks cruised to a 3–0 victory that, in the mug and sweat of a delta day, handed the Tigers their first shutout of the season. Still, those three runs did little to suggest that Shocker batters had cured their RBI anemia. Three years in a row now, WSU bats had fallen faint in the post-season. They had only five hits against Jackson, albeit against some worthy Tiger pitching, which did not inspire much hope.

As it turned out, Jim Thomas and Loren Hibbs, the first two batters in the WSU lineup, produced all the Shocker runs against the hometown University of New Orleans. Jimmy ran the bases Gene's way, thrown out at home trying to score from first base, and Bryan Oelkers took control of a game in a way that only a first-round Major League pitcher could.

The University of New Orleans fans packed the stands, turning the regional into nothing but a home game for UNO, and with every opposing coach's approach to the mound, they shouted with one voice, "Take him out…leave him in…take him out…leave him in"—the youngsters mocking the opponent's dilemma.

But on Saturday, in the eighth inning, when Wichita State pitching coach Brent Kenmitz walked out to speak with Bryan Oelkers, the UNO fans were chanting, "Take him out. Please take him out." The plea had become a scream of sorts, trailing off toward desperation in the face of Bryan's two-hitter and nine strikeouts. His fastballs, coming in at ninety-plus miles an hour, coupled with his corner-catching breaking balls kept the UNO batters off balance. The middle of the New Orleans lineup saw nothing but pitches down and away. At game's 7–0 final, the stats proved wicked. It was the second straight shutout for the Shocks, just five hits given up in two regional games. "We just got a good old-fashioned thrashing," said UNO coach Ron Maestri. "That's as good a pitcher as we've seen all year."

Thunderstorms rose out of the Gulf and proceeded to drench Privateer Park early Sunday, forcing the postponement of the championship game to two o'clock on Monday afternoon. Sophomore Erik Sonberg, ready to walk his 15-3 record to the mound, was confident. "I'll get us out of here," he said.

Erik Sonberg joined Don Heinkel, Brian Oelkers and Stan Brown in producing a stone-cold 0.33 ERA during the New Orleans Regional.

And indeed he did, having given up just four hits when, after 120 pitches, Stan Brown came on in relief in the eighth. Poor Stan. Through no real fault of his own, New Orleans scored a run in the ninth for a final score of Shockers 8, Privateers 1. After twenty-six innings of scoreless baseball, the Shocker staff at last allowed a run. No matter; with their seventieth win, the team had established yet another NCAA record. As the Shockers turned their ambitions toward the College World Series, the pitching staff left New Orleans with a tournament ERA of 0.33. And yes, that decimal point is correct: 0.33!

OMAHA AT LAST

The 1982 College World Series opened on June 4 with a 5:10 p.m. game between Maine and Miami, followed by the Shocks in the nightcap against Cal State–Fullerton. The following afternoon, Oklahoma State would take on Texas, followed by South Carolina and Stanford. From the first pitch, the Shockers proved to be the crowd favorite at Johnny Rosenblatt Stadium, a large pack of the faithful having traveled north to shout their deep-down love of all things black-and-gold baseball. Even the locals displayed their loyalty to the Missouri Valley Conference with a vocal presence that said the Shocks' regular-season manhandling of hometown Creighton mattered not a bit.

A new television network was covering the 1982 CWS, a network predicated on the unlikely notion of wall-to-wall sports, twenty-four hours a day of nothing but ball, albeit many of those hours given over to obscure "Australian Rules Football," an amalgam of rugby and chainsaws that filled late nights and early mornings in those first days of ESPN. The cameras were rolling as the Shockers set about the methodical dismantling of Cal State–Fullerton, continuing the domination of the Titans begun back in Wichita a few days previous.

Bryan Oelkers took the ball and promptly delivered his second straight shutout, running his record to 17-2, a national best, with nineteen straight scoreless innings. He struck out six, including three Ks for the poor Fullerton cleanup hitter, but mostly relied on his breaking ball and off-speed stuff to force Cal State hitters into ground balls and pop flies.

Jimmy Thomas hit the first pitch of the game on a rope into left field, stole second and strode home on Loren Hibbs's rocket off the Fullerton shortstop's glove. Tim Gaskell also continued his quiet efficiency, going four for four from the eight-hole. The 7–0 score might have been much more lopsided, the Shocks leaving men in scoring positions all night long, and Cal State committing five errors, throwing wild pitches and balking—not CWS stuff at all.

And in a karmic moment for sure, WSU athletic director Ted Bredehoft found himself denied access to the ballpark. Scrambling to find a ticket to the game after the NCAA refused to give him a press pass, Bredehoft called here, called there, shouted his right to join the 10,329 fans already inside and only when Shocker graduate assistant Rick Younger gave up his coach's participant pass did Ted at last walk through the gate. "Goes around, comes around," Gene thought maybe for just a moment, remembering those winter days four years previous when his guys were denied admission to the university's own arena, forced off campus to find the old Northside YMCA out of the wind and the cold.

Miami Twice

There were all sorts of ways of looking at Wichita State's 4–3 loss to Miami, a second-round heartbreaker that saw the Shocks strand men on base, saw old reliable Heinkel miss a pitch at just the wrong times, saw error after error in the field, saw Shocker batsmen bring nothing like authority to their swings. Even the run-scoring triples were poorly hit fly balls that barely stayed inside the right-field foul line, easy outs in some ballparks for Loren Hibbs's three-bagger in the first and Dave Lucas's in the fifth. Meanwhile, Miami hitters—Phil Lane, Sam Sorce and Nelson Santovenia in particular—waited on a Don Heinkel pitch to crush. "Very uncharacteristically, Don threw some mistakes," Gene said. "He got badly burned on a few of his throws, but he kept us in the game. We still had a chance to win it in the ninth"—right up until Kevin Penner was picked off base to end it all.

Wichita Eagle staff writer Casey Scott pulled no journalistic punches. "Wichita State had questionable pitching, sloppy defense, and weak hitting," he wrote. "And when the Shockers did get on base, they had little clue about what was going on." Ouch. "Horrendous baserunning," he called it. For example, in the sixth inning, Academic All-American Phil Stephenson fell victim to the tournament's most bizarre play, a hidden-ball deal that would one day find itself made forever notorious as one of ESPN's "25 Biggest Sports Blunders." Ouch. Darn. Ouch again, amid typical *Eagle* negativity. But perhaps the biggest mistake occurred in the eighth inning, when, with no outs, Jim Thomas doubled, only to be picked off by Miami shortstop Bill Wrona.

SHOCKERS 2, BIG EIGHT CONFERENCE 0

The O-State game was pretty much over in the first thirty minutes, as the Shocks sent ten men to the plate in the first inning, five of whom scored. Three hours later, the score stood at 13–2, Erik Sonberg having scattered nine hits while striking out thirteen Cowboys and stretching his season record to 17-3. The more than nine thousand fans in Rosenblatt Stadium saw the Shockers turn a CWS game into, in OSU coach Gary Ward's words, "a laugher."

Erik Sonberg, the WSU starter, watched from the bullpen as his teammates batted and batted some more. Finding it necessary to re-warm his arm before pitching the second inning, Erik fretted. "It's not that I don't appreciate a big lead," he said. "I just have a tendency not to concentrate as much when we get up by big runs early. I'd just as soon have the game closer for a while." Poor Erik. The Shocks continued to shellac the ball, even as he held Oklahoma State hitters to a few scattered singles. Only in the seventh did the Cowboys string some hits together, but by then, the Wichita State lead stood at 11–0, another outburst in the fifth adding six runs to Erik's unwanted lead.

As the Shockers prepared for Texas, who would lose to Miami in a battle of the theretofore unbeaten, Gene spoke of then and now. "Wichita State of May and June is not the team we were in February," the coach insisted. "We are not what you would call a warm-climate team, and we were struggling then. We have yet to score a run against Texas in sixteen innings, and I just hope that it isn't extended to twenty-five innings." No one associated with the UT baseball program expected the drought to continue, nor did they expect the Horns to be eliminated from the series so matter-of-factly, to lose their way back to Austin in fewer than twenty-four hours. The Shockers came out running: Loren Hibbs, batting .556 for the series, singled with one out in the top of the first, stole second and came home on Phil Stephenson's single to right. The Texans understood fast starts, too, scoring two runs of their own in the bottom of the first and hitting WSU starter Bryan Oelkers almost at will. Then Russ Morman pumped a Major League home run, as high as it was far, to open the Shocker third. Eleven more Shocks came to bat that inning, scoring four more runs. WSU 7, Texas 2. The Longhorns would hang around, though, bringing single runs across the plate in the next two innings. Oelkers, still unsettled on the mound and still serving up too many fat ones, surrendered nine hits and six walks on the day but stayed strong, pitching better and better as the three-hour marathon slogged on. "Bryan is a tremendously strong person, both physically and mentally," Gene told reporters later. "Like any great pitcher, if you don't get him early, you ain't gonna get him." And the Longhorns didn't.

The Shockers' elation at beating Texas, the team that had treated them so horribly in their first meetings ten weeks earlier, quieted to silent prayer as they waited word on one of their own. Left fielder Kevin Penner, the intent natural athlete with the Nebraska work ethic, lay in pain, his head swathed in bandages and his future as clouded as his vision.

Here's what happened.

Calvin Schiraldi's catcher had just signaled for a fastball in the second inning, and when Calvin used his entire six-foot-five frame in its delivery, Kevin Penner went down hard, the ball striking him just below his left eye. Texas coach Cliff Gustafson said that Schiraldi's pitch "just got away from him. I think the wild pitch hurt our cause. It fired WSU up, and I think it affected Calvin's pitching at that point. It's just tough for a pitcher to see something like that and think that the other young man might be seriously hurt." Kevin lay in the batter's box for a full ten minutes before a stretcher and then an ambulance arrived to take him to Omaha's St. Joseph Hospital. He was then transferred to University Hospital in Ann Arbor, Michigan, where a team of specialists waited to repair the four broken bones surrounding the eye. His vision returned as the massive swelling receded, but Kevin remained unable to move his eye to the left, even as a complete recovery loomed possible.

There are times when baseball is just a game, and real life, in all its hurt and happenstance, turns off the lights before the stands have emptied.

So Close, So Very Close

The huge photo that dominated the front page of *The Sunflower*, the WSU student newspaper, showed a young woman in tears, WSU bat girl Kathy

Kircher sobbing in the massive arms of WuShock, his smile frozen in disbelief, his great shag of hair soaking up her tears. The Miami Hurricanes, 9; Kathy's beloved Shockers, 3. "Shocks Live, Die by Hustling" read the headline. It was a commentary on both the team's game-to-game philosophy and the last play of the last game, wherein Jim Thomas was called out on his all-out attempt to take third base after a fly out to left field. *The Sunflower* reporter admitted that Jimmy's haul might "have been a foolish attempt for many teams, but it was the style of play that led WSU to an NCAA record seventy-three victories. Their statistics awed the country, but it was aggressiveness which took the Wichita State University Shockers to the finals of the 1982 College World Series."

And as the Shocker mascot shed his first baseball tears in years, it was simply Miami's turn. Turned back for the previous five years in a row, the Hurricanes just couldn't lose against the hard-charging Shockers. Coming from three runs down, the Canes let fly with six of their own in the top of the fifth inning to claim a CWS crown denied them in wholehearted, second-best attempts begun in 1974.

The hurt ran gut deep for Don Heinkel, the ace suffering the two losses in the tournament and, according to his coach, "the most consistently excellent pitcher in collegiate baseball." Don was the man who came into the tournament with a wild-eyed 0.33 ERA, the hero of the regionals whose two wins there brought the Shockers to Rosenblatt Stadium.

Wichita's ABC affiliate, KAKE-TV Channel 10, pre-empted *The Love Boat* and *Fantasy Island*—two goofy television shows whose titles had so very much to do with the Shockers' almost-perfect season—to televise the CWS championship game. And those shows were ready to air after their postponement before Jim Thomas was ready to give up his loud, louder and louder-still discussion with the base umpire who had called him out at third and then had tossed him from the game, as Jimmy became the only baseball player ever to be thrown out of a game after the season was over, indeed after the player's career was over.

"We were the best team there," Gene said, with not a hint of disappointment. A baseball man of the old school, he understands the slips and slides of America's game. And then, with not a hint of disapproval, he wondered aloud, "I'm not sure why Charlie called slider after slider, but I trust his decisions completely. He knows his pitcher better than anyone." This, of course, a reference to the best catcher in the collegiate game at the time, one of the five or ten best catchers ever to play in Division I and the MLB catcher who, in fifteen seasons, caught eleven different Cy

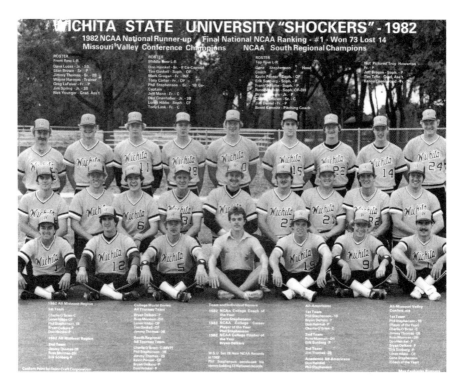

No heartbreak around here. Losing to Miami in the championship game of the College World Series fulfilled an absurd promise made by a workingman named Gene Stephenson.

Young winners, three of them—Roger Clemens, Pat Hentgen and Greg Maddux—in their awarded seasons. That Charlie. Charlie O'Brien who knew perfectly well why he called slider after slider from Don Heinkel.

Five Shockers took their places on the All-College World Series team: Jim Thomas at second base, Tim Gaskell and Loren Hibbs in the outfield, Russ Morman as the designated hitter and Bryan Oelkers as a pitcher. In mid-July, *All-America Baseball News* (now *Baseball America*) named Charlie O'Brien, Phil Stephenson, Bryan Oelkers and Don Heinkel to the magazine's All-America first team and Erik Sonberg, Russ Morman and Jim Thomas to its second team.

As the Shockers looked back over the 1982 season, the disappointment still burning in their throats, the accomplishments of the players and coaches—both as a team and as individuals—demonstrated the differences a year can make. Bryan Oelkers was named the 1982 College Baseball Pitcher of the Year by *All-America Baseball News*, receiving the honor in a class that also included Roger Clemens. Bryan's 1982 statistics (18–2, 2.09 ERA, 166 strikeouts) gleamed in absolute terms and shone like the sun in relative terms, as he led all pitchers in wins, strikeouts and shutouts (six). The Minnesota Twins noticed immediately and took him as the first college pitcher in the MLB draft and the fourth player overall.

Chapter 8
WHAT WE HAVE HERE

Following the 1982 College World Series while writing for the Los Angeles Times–Washington Post News Service, Thomas Boswell offered extended commentary entitled "College Baseball's No Longer a Minor-League Sport," wherein he suggested that "these are the good ol' days for college baseball," foretelling a time when "the pioneers of today's high-quality collegiate game can even begin to see a prosperous maturity." And given his appearance in the piece, it seems that Gene Stephenson was considered among that number, those farsighted pioneers. "It's old news that the overwhelming majority of big leaguers have played at the college level," Mr. Boswell wrote. "At the moment, more than seventy percent of all American-born Major Leaguers have played in college. And that figure keeps rising. Playing in college is not a trend; it's an established, irreversible fact of baseball life."

The columnist sees in the college games a wide-open opportunity for proper instruction in the nuances of the game, much of that teaching individualized. By the summer of 1982, collegiate baseball had become a true team game, "with an emphasis on smart play, hustle, and winning," whereas in the minor leagues, "individual stats become all-important. From the first clank of aluminum bat against ball, it's obvious that the college game is geared toward offense and brains. Because the two most difficult skill positions in baseball—pitcher and catcher—are spread thin in college, many clubs wisely emphasize long-ball hitting and team speed."

And to demonstrate his point, columnist Boswell trots out Wichita State University. "When Coach Gene Stephenson arrived in 1978, the Shockers didn't have a baseball team," he said. "There hadn't been a bat or glove on campus in eight years. The 1982 Shockers were a club of staggering statistics, a team producing 101 home runs and (gulp) 333 stolen bases. The Shockers' Murderers' Row of Phil Stephenson, Russ Morman and Charlie O'Brien had RBI totals of 115, 130 and 116, respectively." The column then cited WSU's performance in the CWS as an indicator of the depth and increasing balance of power in the collegiate ranks: the high draft choices no longer arrive from but a few perennial powerhouses, the Southern Cals and Arizona States of the world. The article called particular attention to then-commissioner of baseball Bowie Kuhn, whom Miami coach Ron Fraser called "college baseball's best friend, most especially in his work to abolish the annual January draft, bringing at last some stability, some predictability to the college game by allowing coaches to rely on players' sticking around for at least three years."

Stability, it seems, was the newest virtue of collegiate baseball, with guys in black and gold playing for the pure, ongoing love of the greatest game in the world.

COACH KEITH HACKETT'S FIRST OVERWHELMING QUESTION

Baker University did not exactly present a challenge to the Shockers when the two teams met in April 1982 in a double-header taken by WSU 17–0 and 12–0, aces Don Heinkel and Erik Sonberg shutting out the Wildcats while Shocker batsmen teed off for almost thirty runs in foreshortened games, a total of ten innings, in fact. Baker coach Keith Hackett spoke sanguinely about the whole deal: "I figured if I was going to get bombed, I would get bombed close to home, where I wouldn't have to spend a lot of money for travel." Coach Hackett admired Gene's guys' prowess. "They were tremendous," he said. "They hit the ball hard, and they hit it anywhere. It's funny, because when I talked to Gene, he told me he didn't think his team was as good offensively as last year. And their pitchers were great. I bet they have fourteen or fifteen pitchers who could pitch for us." Fourteen or fifteen?

It was perhaps with those exaggerations in mind that Coach Hackett moved on to speculation about WSU baseball and its finances. "I'd be interested to know their budget," he said. "I bet he [Gene] spends more for bats than I do for my entire team." (Fact: all WSU bats were donated; no money out of the budget for the Worths and Eastons.) Strange that a coach from the heavily endowed, high-tuition Baker University should want to talk money with a Division I sports program in but the fifth year of its resurgence. Surely Coach Keith Hackett knew of the Shocks relative rags-to-riches story, but in any case, he posed the money question, and admirably, WSU officials did not spare the details of the bucks and their origin. There was an operating budget of $120,000 for the baseball program, a university spokesman dutifully reported. The budget had more than doubled in five years, years in which the Shockers had risen to national prominence on a trajectory roughly that of a Saturn rocket. That said, the Shockers still came by their bucks the hard way. A team having shown itself fully equipped to win it all was still holding raffles for sides of beef and chances on a trip to Las Vegas, for goodness sake. Furthermore, Wichita State baseball "gets a cut of basketball gate receipts and, of course, basketball is our biggest moneymaker," said Kevin Weiberg, WSU sports information director.

Baker University's inquiry into high finance in Kansas baseball prompted a comparison with another basketball school, the state's largest university up in Lawrence, where varsity baseball occurred with an outlay of about $190,000, a bit more than Gene's' first-year, 1978 budget on which to build a program from scratch. Still, the question begged for an answer regarding the budget comparison between two schools that were so very different otherwise. For starters, Gene Stephenson had the temerity to charge admission to Shocker games even in that first, formative year, when he hauled tarps from the football stadium to drape over the makeshift fence that, Gene hoped, would set paying customers apart from freeloading passersby. For that season-ending series against Cal State–Fullerton, Gene charged a fat four dollars for a seat to see two top-ten teams have it out. And all the while he campaigned for individual and corporate support of his burgeoning program, delivering on his promise to show the homefolk some young men who came to play.

Coach Keith Hackett's Second Overwhelming Question

Now came a second inquiry belonging to Baker coach Keith Hackett, a surpassing strange question on the occasion of his team's being shut out by thirty runs by a baseball team whose finances and whose academics he questioned.

"When do they go to school?" he wondered aloud. It was a little smug maybe, the question coming from a coach at a small liberal arts college. However, it was understandable in the context of the Shockers' everlasting schedule, eighty-seven eventual games for the '82 season, half of what the big leagues play and more than any other collegiate team in history. And Mr. Hackett's bemusement at Shocker ballplayers' academic records was hardly the first public commentary on the meaning of "student-athlete" in the baseball program. "We've taken a lot of flak from academicians—from our president on down—about the number of games we play," Gene admitted, just before he pointed out that his scholars had the highest grade-point average of any sports team at Wichita State, golf and tennis included. Most starters boasted GPAs well above 3.0—this included Don Heinkel and Phil Stephenson, both of whom would be named first-team Academic All-Americans, Don in fact winning an NCAA scholarship for postgraduate work in medical school.

Gene took pains to assemble his schedule around the demands of the classroom and the study hall, all home games starting mid-afternoon or, when down at Lawrence-Dumont Stadium, under the lights. Road trips were concentrated on weekends and during breaks in the semester. "These players work hard in the classroom," their coach insisted. "If a player doesn't go to class, then he doesn't play. These guys are here to get an education."

WHAT GENE HAS DONE

One of the greatest college baseball coaches of all time, J. Stanley "Skip" Bertman recently moved from his seven-year position as athletic director at Louisiana State University into what LSU administrators called "a vital fundraising role." Today, Coach Bertman remains one of college baseball's most known and most respected figures. In his two decades in the dugout at LSU, Skip guided the Tigers to five NCAA titles, with LSU drawing more fans than any other baseball program in the country. He led Team USA to the bronze medal in the 1996 Atlanta Olympics. Coach Bertman is an inaugural member of the National College Baseball Hall of Fame, the Louisiana Sports Hall of Fame and the American Baseball Coaches Association Hall of Fame. As LSU's athletic director, he managed a budget in excess of $50 million.

And so heads turn when Skip Bertman says, "No one in college baseball has done what Gene has accomplished at Wichita State University." No qualifying ifs, ands or buts. "Gene had no friends in high places; in fact, university administration was at first lukewarm at best toward the renewed baseball program. In the early days, no one donor stepped forward with a major gift— please understand, Gene worked hard to get grassroots support all around— he built that sort of support, as hundreds of Wichitans stepped forward to help as they could, but I'm talking here of the sort of boosterism like Boone Pickens at Oklahoma State or Nike at the University of Oregon. Gene had none of that. He put in his own sprinkler system. Come on now." Skip continues:

> *Gene could pull players out of the stands and find a way to beat you. He found these young men and then coached them into his system. And he has truly built a system, a program, a tradition—not many coaches survive thirty-five years at any school in any sport. Terry Jolly and Brent Kenmitz and Jim Thomas and Billy Hall and Loren Hibbs have all shown such loyalty to Gene and to the program. Even with all the unavoidable disadvantages that still confront the program, from the cold weather to the relative weakness of the Missouri Valley Conference—all due respect here, it's just that these smaller northern schools do not, will not ever have the resources of the huge BCS universities.*

After he left WSU in 1982, the NCAA record for single-season runs scored in his bat bag, Loren Hibbs played for a short time in the San Francisco Giants farm system. After the slow realization that "I wasn't good enough to play at the Major League level," Loren came home to serve as a WSU assistant coach from 1987 to 1992. He then went on to take the managerial helm at the University of North Carolina–Charlotte in 1993, averaging all this time more than thirty wins a season. Of course, he had stood at Gene's side in 1989, the championship season, the year the Shockers won it all, and he speaks of that experience as transformative: "I would not be coaching at Charlotte without the guidance Gene has provided over the years. He allowed me the freedom to work and give my input. The two things that come immediately to mind when I think of Gene are his intense desire to compete and the continuity of his staff. No one has accomplished what he has in our profession—building a nationally competitive program from scratch at a non-BCS school in a cold-weather climate while raising millions of dollars in support of the program and developing a big bunch of guys who have gone on to play in the Majors."

Jim Thomas, now a longtime coach at WSU, speaks of other sorts of stability: "We recruit players with professional aspirations. We tell these young men that we'll develop their skills. We'll make them complete players, ready for the next stage in their baseball careers. At the same time, we tell players that if they're looking for TGIF and fraternities and tailgate parties before big football games—college life ahead of baseball—well then, we're probably not the school for them." And nothing is about to change. "Thirty-five years later, and our practices are still the same—the same drills and the same emphasis on meaningful, game-speed repetition," Coach Thomas says.

UNAFRAID AND GUTS ABLAZE

Now a community barely maintaining its five-figure residential base, but still a National Historic Landmark, the Guthrie Chamber of Commerce lists "championship athletic teams" on its website. The Guthrie High School website, home of the Blue Jays, lists just two notable alumni: Gene and Phil Stephenson. Brothers. Baseball players. Guys who might saddle up for a land rush.

He felt it first on the sandbur-filled schoolyards, the desire to encounter this game with some rigor and some fun. The seasons blurring in the hard dust of this little Okie town, Gene Stephenson played baseball until it was time to play football, the red-dirt way it has always been around here—all hard work, the carnival coming but once a year. Say what you mean; mean what you say. With whiskers starting to grow through the muscle in the jaw, there's no time for talking trash. Put up or shut up.

He ran hard and hit hard at the University of Missouri, a football scholarship his ticket to Columbia, where he started as team captain in right field for the baseball team. A unanimous all-conference player, he led the Big Eight in hitting. Then he was graduated and gone. Vietnam was still hot then, the Tet Offensive swinging the odds against our guys in green. Gene did his duty in the jungle after Germany and its fateful meeting with a fellow baseball coach named Dedeaux. He came home to Oklahoma and waited for the phone to ring. And when it did, he thought once more of baseball's innocence, its naïve belief that all things remain possible in an eternal springtime. And he found again in Kansas young men as he had been—unafraid and driven—who bought into a national collegiate championship in five years' time. It was preposterous stuff, an unthinkable prospect but for two truths underneath it all.

"Let youngsters have fun while they develop their natural abilities." The coach, aging now, his last years in his profession upon him, says again, "Let them develop. Let them enjoy their youth and their growth."

And then, his own coaching come round at last to a final inning or two, he rolls the game he loves into a ball, a ragged old Rawlings, its stitches pinked after a thousand flights into a late afternoon sun. He makes baseball life, and life this nation's game, and he says again to others who'd do as he has done.

"Teach them to play fearlessly," he says. "Teach them to play fearlessly."

ADDENDUM

The page has turned. Gene Stephenson is no longer the baseball coach at Wichita State University. As Coach Stephenson moves on to his next self-directed challenge, a look back demonstrates his likely unmatchable place in the college game.

We begin with winning. Gene was the first NCAA head coach in the 154-year history of collegiate baseball to win 1,800 Division I games, and it now seems almost impossible that any living coach can win so many games in so few years. Gene stands among only three coaches to have achieved as much, but those other two coaches won a significant portion of their games in lower, less competitive divisions. Only five coaches have achieved as many as 1,500 wins at any level of baseball.

Next we turn to percentages. Only two coaches in the history of NCAA baseball have ever won more than 1,500 games while maintaining a winning percentage in excess of .700. No other active coaches are within 350 games of this astronomical level, and the two retired coaches with high winning percentages won 400 fewer games. During Gene's thirty-six seasons, WSU averaged 51 wins per year.

These winning ways have translated to twenty-eight NCAA post-season appearances, seven College World Series appearances, four NCAA College World Series championship finals and, in 1989, the NCAA College World Series Championship itself. Gene's Shockers also won twenty-six Missouri Valley Conference championships, including the 2013 title in his last season at the helm. He left Wichita State with a final record of 1,837-675 for a masterful .731 winning percentage.

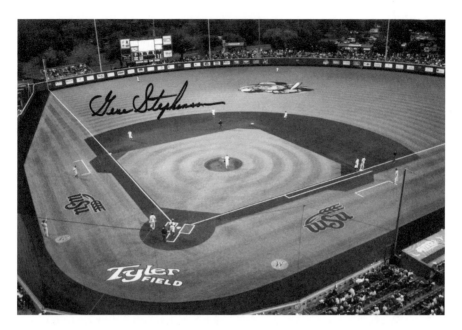

Like the hundreds of young men he coached, Gene Stephenson left nothing on the field at game's end.

Coach Stephenson's knowledge of the game, his relentless demands on the practice field and his proven abilities to motivate young men have sent thirty-three former Shockers to the Majors and have produced fifty-four All-Americans and twenty-seven Academic All-Americans, the last a number that leads the NCAA in all divisions. (Notre Dame is a distant second.)

The lessons remain: play fearlessly, practice hard to play hard and, as Coach Stephenson learned as a little boy on a tilt-a-whirl in a dust-blown Okie town, enjoy the ride.

INDEX

ABOUT THE AUTHOR

During his career as a freelance writer and ghostwriter, John Brown has completed almost five thousand writing assignments, including six biographies and corporate histories. *Wichita State Baseball Comes Back* is his most recent work. He and his wife, Lee Ann, split their time between Wichita and their ranch in the Flint Hills.